You Have to Go to School—
You're the **Principal!**

For my wife and daughters

Gertrude, Katie, and Mary Ellen Young

May they find as much fulfillment in their chosen fields of work as I have in mine.

And for my mentors, colleagues, and friends who have time after time demonstrated these tips to be wise and helpful.

You Have to Go to School— You're the Principal!

101 Tips
to Make It Better for Your Students, Your Staff, and Yourself

Paul G. Young

Foreword by Vincent Ferrandino

CORWIN PRESS
A Sage Publications Company
Thousand Oaks, California

Copyright © 2004 by Corwin Press

All rights reserved. When forms and sample documents are included, their use is authorized only by educators, local school sites, and/or noncommercial entities who have purchased the book. Except for that usage, no part of this book may be reproduced or utilized in any form or by any means, electronic or mechanical, including photocopying, recording, or by any information storage and retrieval system, without permission in writing from the publisher.

For information:

Corwin Press
A Sage Publications Company
2455 Teller Road
Thousand Oaks, California 91320
www.corwinpress.com

Sage Publications Ltd.
1 Oliver's Yard
55 City Road
London EC1Y 1SP
United Kingdom

Sage Publications India Pvt. Ltd.
B-42, Panchsheel Enclave
Post Box 4109
New Delhi 110 017 India

Printed in the United States of America

Library of Congress Cataloging-in-Publication Data

Young, Paul, 1950-
 You have to go to school—you're the principal! : 101 tips to make it better for your students, your staff, and yourself / by Paul Young.
   p. cm.
 Includes bibliographical references.
   ISBN 1-4129-0471-4 (cloth) — ISBN 1-4129-0472-2 (pbk.)
 1. School principals—United States. 2. School management and organization—United States. I. Title.
 LB2831.92.Y68 2004
 371.2'012—dc22
                                                    2004004598

04 05 06 07 08 10 9 8 7 6 5 4 3 2 1

Acquisitions Editor:	Jean Ward
Production Editor:	Kristen Gibson
Copy Editor:	Marilyn Power Scott
Typesetter:	C&M Digitals (P) Ltd.
Proofreader:	Sally Scott

Contents

Foreword   xi

Preface   xiii

About the Author   xv

Introduction   1

1. Leadership   5
   - Tip 1: Focus on Children   6
   - Tip 2: Be Courageous   7
   - Tip 3: Model Learning   9
   - Tip 4: Understand the Levels of Leadership   10
   - Tip 5: Foster Good Relations With the Support Staff   13
   - Tip 6: Delegate   14
   - Tip 7: Never Underestimate the Importance of a Managerial Task   15
   - Tip 8: Always Be People Oriented   16
   - Tip 9: Know People's Names   18
   - Tip 10: Show Restraint   20
   - Tip 11: Lead Regular Tours of the School   22
   - Tip 12: Give Bonuses   23
   - Tip 13: Become a Mastermind Thinker   24
   - Tip 14: Buy Time   25
   - Tip 15: Have a Security Plan in Place   27
   - Tip 16: Memorize the Negotiated Agreements   28
   - Tip 17: Never Try to Conceal Big Problems   29
   - Tip 18: Never Shoot the Messenger   30

2. Vision — 31
- Tip 19: Establish High Expectations — 32
- Tip 20: Develop Effective, Challenging Goals — 34
- Tip 21: Know the Trends in Education — 36
- Tip 22: Determine Your Fundamental Beliefs About Education — 39
- Tip 23: Take Risks and Learn From Mistakes — 43
- Tip 24: Be Decisive and Take Action — 45
- Tip 25: Embrace Diversity — 46
- Tip 26: Don't Ride Dead Horses — 47

3. Student Learning — 49
- Tip 27: Never Underestimate the Importance of Instructional Leadership — 50
- Tip 28: Understand the Child of Poverty — 52
- Tip 29: Be a Curriculum Leader — 54
- Tip 30: Make Morning Announcements — 55
- Tip 31: Eat Lunch With the Students — 57
- Tip 32: Support the Arts — 58
- Tip 33: Support All Extracurricular Activities — 60
- Tip 34: Focus on Discipline by Teaching, Not Punishing — 62
- Tip 35: Determine How You'll Make Classroom Placements — 64
- Tip 36: Learn What's Special About Special Education — 66
- Tip 37: Master Conflict Resolution Skills — 68
- Tip 38: Visit Three Classrooms Each Day — 69
- Tip 39: Take Pictures Regularly — 70
- Tip 40: Organize a Student Council — 71

4. Adult Learning — 73
- Tip 41: Hire Good People and Invest in Them to Keep Them — 74
- Tip 42: Staff Development Must Be Ongoing — 77
- Tip 43: Give Your Superstars What They Need and Let Them Fly — 79

Tip 44: Don't Squash Others' Ideas	81
Tip 45: Learn How to Ask Questions	83
Tip 46: Avoid District Politics	85
Tip 47: Run Effective Meetings	87
Tip 48: Keep the Monkeys on the Backs of Others	89
Tip 49: Encourage Consensus Decision Making	92

5. Data — **95**

Tip 50: Collect, Manage, Analyze, and Use Data to Drive Decisions	96
Tip 51: Use Tests for Diagnostic Purposes	98
Tip 52: Reduce Paper Use	99
Tip 53: Help Teachers Become Data Users	101
Tip 54: Use Technology	103

6. Parents and Community — **105**

Tip 55: Engage the Community	106
Tip 56: Be the Cheerleader for Your School	108
Tip 57: Be Accountable and Advocate for School Resources	109
Tip 58: Maintain a Current Web Site for the School	110
Tip 59: Develop a Repertoire of Parent Involvement Activities	112
Tip 60: Learn How to Work With the Media	115
Tip 61: Collect and Tell Stories	117
Tip 62: Talk to Lawmakers	118
Tip 63: Be Active in Your Community	120
Tip 64: Call 911 When Necessary	121
Tip 65: Listen	123
Tip 66: Celebrate Successes	125
Tip 67: Encourage an International Perspective	127

7. Taking Care of the Organization — **129**

Tip 68: Don't Overlook the Little Details	130
Tip 69: Organize the Office	133
Tip 70: Read and Respond to E-Mail	135

Tip 71: Return All Phone Messages the Same Day	137
Tip 72: Write Notes Daily	138
Tip 73: Keep a Special Idea File	139
Tip 74: Maintain Eye Contact	140
Tip 75: Don't Write Memos While Angry	142
Tip 76: Know the Law	144
Tip 77: Ride Your School Buses	145
Tip 78: Recognize Spouses and Family Members	147
Tip 79: Always Make the Superintendent Look Good	148
Tip 80: Become an Authority on Head Lice, Rashes, Infectious Diseases, and Medications	150
Tip 81: Maintain the Highest Level of Character	152
Tip 82: Tell the Truth	154
Tip 83: Smile	155
Tip 84: Have a Sense of Humor	156
Tip 85: Think and Behave Positively	157
Tip 86: Show Pride and Passion for the Principalship	158

8. Taking Care of Yourself — **161**

Tip 87: Keep Fit	162
Tip 88: Don't Smoke	163
Tip 89: Develop a Winning Attitude	164
Tip 90: Arrive Early, Go Home Early—Even if You Take Work Home	165

9. Professional Growth — **167**

Tip 91: Find a Mentor	168
Tip 92: Avoid the Status Quo Syndrome	170
Tip 93: Keep Your Portfolio and Résumé Current	171
Tip 94: Develop a Professional, Collegial Network	172
Tip 95: Read	174
Tip 96: Write	175
Tip 97: Improve Your Speaking Skills	176

Tip 98: Give Professional Presentations	179
Tip 99: Collaborate With Colleagues	180
Tip 100: Invest in Professional Attire	181
Tip 101: Join Your State and National Professional Associations	183
The Principals' Creed	**185**
Suggested Readings	**187**

Foreword

Whether you have just picked up the keys to your first school or you've been a principal for decades, the common sense and heartfelt suggestions from Paul Young should be required—and fast—reading for every school leader. Of course I am delighted with Paul's concluding tip that sings the praises of national and state professional associations, but he covers so much more, from what to wear and how to organize your office to how to make the best impression, get the support staff on your side, and remember the names of every child in your school. And he'll even tell you how *not to burn your bridges* on a very bad day. This little book is packed with good ideas, and reading it doesn't take up too much of your extremely busy day.

The best part is, these solid tips remain constant over time and will be just as meaningful each time you pick up the book.

Dr. Vincent Ferrandino
Executive Director
National Association of
Elementary School Principals

Preface

This book is designed to help elementary and middle level principals. It is intended for the following readers:

- Students and faculty engaged in college-university administrative training programs
- Aspiring principals
- Practicing principals
- Assistant principals
- Retired principals
- Association leaders
- Boards of education
- Superintendents, assistant superintendents
- Directors, supervisors, educational support personnel
- Service industry personnel
- Teachers
- Interested constituencies

This book is a collection of ideas and recommendations for any individual serving as principal in an elementary or middle level school anywhere in the world. No beginner could master all of these right away, but repertoires will expand with experience. I hope that reading this book will help you reflect and stretch your thinking. Each of you will encounter and identify with the meaning of these tips in your very own special way. That is the way it should be. These recommendations are intended as a guide to success, a source of reflection and discussion, and a handbook that can be used over and over for support as you strive to continuously improve your performance.

About the Author

Paul Young, PhD, is the Principal of West Elementary School in Lancaster, Ohio. He began his career thirty years ago as a high school band director and then, after eleven years, retrained as an elementary school teacher and principal. He taught fourth grade before accepting his first principalship in 1986.

He served as President of the Ohio Association of Elementary School Administrators in 1997 and was elected to the National Association of Elementary School Principals (NAESP) Board of Directors in 1998 (the only person ever elected by write-in ballot), representing Zone 3 until 2001. He became President-elect in 2001 and began his duties as President in July 2002.

Young believes strongly in the importance of the arts in a well-balanced school. He also stresses the importance of aspiring principals programs and the development of mentoring programs (such as NAESP's PALS Corps) for the next generation of principals. He strives to focus national attention on these areas: (1) restructuring of the principalship, (2) rekindling respect for the role of the principalship and public education, (3) expanding the principal's roles of building manager and instructional leader to include community leadership, and (4) developing student-friendly alternatives to the high-stakes testing currently engulfing schools across the nation.

Dr. Young completed his degrees at Ohio University–Athens. He is an adjunct professor of music at Ohio University–Lancaster. His wife, Gertrude, is a vocal and instrumental music teacher with Lancaster City Schools. They are proud parents of two daughters: Katie, a graduate of the Eastman School of Music/University of Rochester and Rice University in Houston, Texas, who recently accepted a position as oboist with the New World Symphony in Miami. Mary Ellen is a senior business-marketing major at the University of Cincinnati and is very active in leadership roles with her sorority, Chi Omega.

Introduction

Principals always want to better themselves. They commit themselves to children and work steadfastly to ensure that each child in their care benefits from a quality education. They wield more influence and social power in their communities than they stop to realize. They represent what is best about education throughout the United States. They are key to everything positive that happens in their schools.

Aspiring principals are ambitious and want to learn and equip themselves with as much information as possible to attain their goals. They studiously complete all their projects and papers in graduate school. They've read all they can about the work of a principal. They've observed. If they were fortunate, they were provided authentic experiences during internships. But once they become principals, accept the keys to a school, and venture into the real world, the learning curve suddenly becomes much higher. Reality hits! Everyone wants to tell them how to do their job—especially those who have never been principals. Some new principals become overwhelmed and discouraged. Others recognize they can gain the edge and survive by learning from effective practitioners.

This book is designed to be an easy read for practicing principals, those who are aspiring, and those who are contemplating careers as principals.

My hope is that reading this book will provide or affirm ideas and insights that will support reflection, professional growth, and career advancement. It is structured as a series of 101 tips that are based on my experience, learning from others, common sense, and observation of the work habits of effective principals. They are presented in short, simple statements and stories. They are not based on scientific research. They reflect my opinions.

This book is also intended as a vehicle for sharing best practices among all principals. The first six chapters of the book are related to the standards articulated by the National Association for Elementary School Principals (NAESP) in its 2001 publication, *Leading Learning Communities: Standards for What Principals Should Know and Be Able To Do*. This best-selling document defines, clarifies, and presents a rubric for instructional leadership, the primary role of principals. The standards were developed by principals for principals—just as doctors establish standards for their professional work. Principals from across the nation contributed to this excellent tool for new and veteran principals to use for reflection and self-evaluation. As outlined in the six standards, effective leaders

- Lead schools in a way that places student and adult learning at the center
- Set high expectations and standards for the academic and social development of all students and the performance of adults
- Demand content and instruction that ensure student achievement of agreed-on academic standards
- Create a culture of continuous learning for adults tied to student learning and other school goals
- Use multiple sources of data as diagnostic tools to assess, identify, and apply instructional improvement
- Actively engage the community to create shared responsibility for student and school success

In the NAESP document, each of the foregoing standards is summarized by a single word or short phrase: leadership, vision, student learning, adult learning, data and decision making, and community engagement, respectively. These key words for the six standards have been adopted for the first six categories of tips. Thus,

Chapter 1: Leadership

Chapter 2: Vision

Chapter 3: Student Learning

Chapter 4: Adult Learning

Chapter 5: Data

Chapter 6: Parents and Community

The tips in Chapters 1 through 6 are not intended as an exhaustive roadmap to achievement of those standards but as a set of efficacy builders and entry points for leaders to improve practice in each of the targeted areas. For a fully realized reflective tool for growth, no principal will want to be without the NAESP standards document. These tips are offered to open ways for principals to focus on specifics and target one small area for improvement at a time.

Even recognizing the primacy of instructional leadership, principals need to address other aspects of the principal's role that are crucial to professional success and satisfaction. It is managing the whole job day in and day out with efficiency and integrity that enables principals to keep in sight and accomplish the work that brought them into the profession: ensuring the quality education of children. Chapters 7 through 9 include tips to support the principal in three essentials of this endeavor:

Chapter 7: Taking Care of the Organization

Chapter 8: Taking Care of Yourself

Chapter 9: Professional Growth

A reader of this book may find a different emphasis in one or more of these tips and may be inclined to mentally move it to another section. That's fine. Many of the tips support more than one purpose, and nothing would please me more than to think a reader might adapt a tip to address a different professional priority.

Many of the tips are applicable not only for principals' professional work but for their personal lives as well. They will help an administrator become a more effective leader. Many tips are time honored and have passed through generations of mentors. The list presented is not all inclusive. Following these tips does not guarantee success in the principalship but should lead to an acknowledged level of competence and effectiveness.

Remember that nothing effective can happen in an elementary or middle level school unless it has the endorsement and support of the principal. The principal sets the tone for everything. These 101 tips will help principals set that tone and make their schools a place people want to come to, a better, richer place for learning for students, staff, parents, the community—and the principal.

1
Leadership

If the first button of one's coat is wrongly buttoned, all the rest will be crooked.

—Giordano Bruno

Tip 1

Focus on Children

This tip is Number 1 for principals. It is the lens through which all tips, programs, action, and reflection should filter and against which all should be measured. First and last, maintain a focus on children. It's simple, too often overlooked, but critically important. In everything you do, if you consider the impact on and the benefits for children, you won't go wrong.

May a focus on children become your defining force!

Tip 2

Be Courageous

If you aren't a brave person, don't consider becoming a principal. If you can't stand the sight of blood or broken bones, forget it! Principals of the twenty-first century must be models of mental and moral strength; capable of venturing into the unknown; persevering; and able to withstand fear, difficulty, danger, and attacks—both physical and emotional. Courage is an essential ingredient of being a school leader, especially a progressive leader.

Ernest Hemingway described courage as "grace under pressure." Courageous principals maintain their cool under fire. These individuals aren't afraid of angry parents. They make home visits. Keeping kids' best interests in mind, they recognize the political ramifications of decisions they know they must make—and they make them anyway. Courageous principals are those who put others' safety interests before their own.

The world watched the horrific events of September 11, 2001, unfold on television. But what they missed seeing were the untold courageous acts and the quick decisions made by principals, not only in New York City and Washington, DC, but also throughout the nation. Immediately, principals' thoughts focused on the safety of others, particularly students. Those closest to the scenes of the terrorist attacks calmly evacuated schools, making sure children safely made it into the care of parents or guardians. New York City principals made sure every child was safe, accounted for, and safely delivered to a responsible adult. Likewise in Washington, DC, and other close areas. Those farther away began helping people cope, understand, and attend to those in need. They aided in preventing widespread panic and retribution against people with Middle Eastern backgrounds. Principals in Washington, DC, Maryland, and Virginia helped students and citizens survive treacherous days in late 2002 as the DC sniper terrorized their communities. These examples are high-profile, emergency situations familiar to most everyone. But there are countless others happening all too often throughout the nation. Through them all, there have been courageous principals modeling calm, reasonable responses and helping children address their fears and anxieties.

Today, like no other time before, principals must be able to assure anxious parents that their children will be safe at school. They must be prepared to respond to and deal with fires, earthquakes, tornadoes, civil unrest, domestic fights, medical emergencies, drug busts, gas leaks, sexual predators, and wild and crazy people in their neighborhoods.

The principalship is not for the faint of heart!

Tip 3

Model Learning

"Effective principals lead their schools in a way that places student and adult learning at the center" (NAESP, 2001, *Leading Learning Communities: Standards for What Principals Should Know and Be Able To Do*, p. 9). As an instructional leader, the principal is always learning. By this example, students and adults alike are continuously learning. When adults stop learning, so will students.

Enroll in postgraduate classes. Attend workshops, seminars, and inservice meetings. Many opportunities are available online to accommodate busy schedules. Be a regular attendee at state and national professional conferences for principals. Read books. Organize book clubs and study groups at school. Talk about new ideas with friends and colleagues. Show the kind of enthusiasm for learning you would like to see from your students.

Show that learning can be fun. Learn something new each day. The principal sets the tone.

Tip 4

Understand the Levels of Leadership

Despite all the recent attention given instructional leadership, principals frequently find themselves in situations where they simply have to LEAD! The No Child Left Behind Act's "Adequate Yearly Progress" and related requirements have serious accountability consequences for principals. Traditional approaches to working with staffs, parents, and students must be reconsidered for effectiveness. In those schools being labeled as failing according to the NCLB Act, improvement may not begin until attitudes and beliefs about student learning are changed. That improvement will require a leader. Change can be good but often is difficult for insecure and ineffective classroom performers. To realize improvement, the principal must lead, and the activities and process will be far different than managing or instructional leadership.

Author John Maxwell, in his book *Leadership 101*, provides a clear outline of the progressive levels of leadership. He lists five levels of leadership, as follows:

1. Position
2. Permission
3. Production
4. People Development
5. Personhood

When first selected for the principalship, rookies find themselves at the position level. Unfortunately, some never progress farther. They have a title, become complacent, fall into a rut, assume they have "arrived," and arrogantly fail to do anything with the title. They wonder why they can't make things happen in their schools.

Maxwell points out that leaders must progress naturally through the five levels, warning not to skip a level. That is the mistake I made!

Like those who thought they had arrived, when being selected for a principalship, I failed to gain permission from my staff to become their leader. I began expecting results, a third-level outcome—skipping level 2. My efforts were ineffective and my frustration intense until I learned the importance of building relationships with those who wanted a leader. I am indebted to my mentors for their redirection.

Once a person has been accepted and solidified permission to become the principal and to lead, much like a husband and wife must establish their close interpersonal relationship, the principal can eventually move up to the third level, production. Couples start families at this level, and principals and their staffs begin to realize the fruits of their work together. Progress is made, results are data driven, and improvement is continuous. Fear, if it exists, is at minimal levels. People grow together. Teachers teach and students learn. The principal fulfills the role of instructional leadership.

Moving higher, effective principals strive to build a strong team. They empower others and delegate effectively. They focus on developing people and surround themselves with superstars. They invest time in helping others become effective leaders. They fully realize their influence, reach out, and help others fulfill their dreams. They maintain high expectations and consistently achieve results.

The special few reach the fifth level of leadership, personhood. They understand that sustaining their work can best be accomplished by grooming a successor. Succession planning becomes a focus of their work. These are the principals who are held in such high regard that people assume they cannot be replaced. People are surprised when the successor, who was being quietly trained by an expert leader, makes a smooth transition. Principals who reach the personhood level of leadership sometimes have the school named after them when they retire.

As Maxwell warns, don't try to skip a level. Also, never neglect the components of the lower levels. Furthermore, you must always pick an appropriate level to interact with subordinates and always know what level each employee has attained.

Leadership is all about influence—nothing more, nothing less. To lead our schools to higher levels, principals must first know themselves; work to gain influence; and understand the process, pitfalls, path, and levels of leadership. Learning and gaining influence never stops.

Always work to become a better leader.

Tip 5

Foster Good Relations With the Support Staff

I value the opportunities to talk with my custodians, cooks, and secretary. They help ground me and provide valuable insights about the school and the community. When empowered to do their jobs, they can assume innumerable managerial responsibilities, freeing me as principal to focus on instruction and student learning.

My first superintendent told me that classified employees could make or break me as a beginning principal. It was sage advice. These great workers shared their experience and expertise and enabled me to learn the infrastructure of the school. I deliberately worked to build a close, positive, working relationship with each of them. Together, we grew to value one another and became a team. The superintendent's advice was good, heard, and heeded. I've made it a priority to develop good relationships wherever I've worked.

I've observed and interacted with classified employees who felt they were second-class citizens. When they feel this way, their work production sags and morale suffers. Some even sabotage the leadership efforts of the principal. They talk. Negative stories start spreading through the community. A downward spiral occurs in the relationship with the principal that is sometimes impossible to reverse.

Pay forward. Build relationships with the support staff. When they like you, but more important, respect you, they will be there for you in a time of need.

Tip 6

Delegate

Principals try to be superhuman. They try to do it all. It's impossible.

Learn to empower your staff, classified as well as certified, to make decisions at the most appropriate level of the organization. Allow people to chair committees, make decisions, and complete tasks that can be done without your direct involvement. When people realize that they are being asked to complete tasks or assignments that you would otherwise do yourself, they will help. However, if they perceive that they are being given the dirty jobs, they will of course resist.

Certain responsibilities can be delegated to volunteers. Make sure you explain clearly the objective of the task and how you would like to see things done and provide a time clarification. Volunteers can be an invaluable asset to a principal. Show them your appreciation.

Delegation must be balanced: Too much, and people will think you are trying to get out of work; not enough, and you'll eventually burn out. Approach people like a dictator and they'll sabotage the work.

Learn to delegate. Clearly explain your position and what you envision happening in the school. Use your best people skills, build a team, and create a high-performing school with everyone contributing to the effort.

Tip 7

Never Underestimate the Importance of a Managerial Task

As principal, you are held accountable for everything that happens in your school. Don't delegate away managerial tasks to the point that you have no idea what is happening there.

Understand the infrastructure, procedures, how things work, and what it takes to get things done. If the managing custodian was unable to be at work suddenly, would you know how to open the school? Could you complete a purchase order if your secretary was not available? Could you turn off the gas in the kitchen if you suddenly smelled a leak? Do you know what is involved with stripping floor wax and thoroughly cleaning a restroom? Would you allow students to stand in extreme morning cold if those empowered to bring them inside were slow to act?

Administrators who delegate away their responsibility, who fail to understand what others are to do, are viewed as incapable by staff and parents when a problem surfaces that eventually is brought to the principal to solve. Empower others to do their jobs, but make sure you know how to do their work if they suddenly can't and you need to do it yourself.

Tip 8

Always Be People Oriented

Effective principals have great people skills. They genuinely like people of all ages. They can walk in a room and command positive attention. They possess communication skills that make others feel they are interested in them. They are fun to be around.

Devote a file to collecting information about people in and around the school community. Use a computer, palm pilot, or any other record-keeping system that fits your needs. Collect information about the people you meet, items of special interest, birthdays, information about children, and so on. Clip items from the newspaper, make copies, and send the original with a note to that person. Use the gathered information regularly when talking with people. Ask questions about what you collected. People will be impressed and know you care. Call people on the phone with good news more often than bad.

Greet visitors in your office as though they are each the most important person you will meet all day. They are! They are your customers. Smile, and engage them in conversations. Make sure they leave your office with what they will consider to have been the ultimate customer experience. The next time they come back, they'll be remembering a positive experience.

Talk to those who work in your school. Acknowledge their work and contribution to the school. Talk to the kids. Ask them questions about their families, their interests, what they are learning, and make them feel important.

Not all people are comfortable initiating conversations. Work at it. Make it a goal. The more you focus on improving your people skills—making eye contact, engaging people in positive conversations, and smiling—the easier it becomes. Eventually it will become second nature and become part of your persona.

Many people view the principal as an authoritarian figure. Principals often have to say no and deny people what they want. Those who are people oriented develop ways to soften this perception while delivering the same messages. People who might not always be satisfied by what they hear from the principal will still respect the individual because they perceived that he or she liked them and cared.

Tip 9

Know People's Names

My school has over 400 students and a mobility rate of nearly twenty-five percent. After thirty years in the business, I'll see people on the street that might have been in one of my marching bands, my fourth-grade classes, or a school where I've served as principal. My strength is in remembering faces, not names.

People love it when you can address them by their names, first as well as last. When they recognize that you also know something about them, it further validates their individuality and strengthens your relationship with them. Students gain your acceptance and feel they belong in "your" school. I have to work at remembering names.

I work at it by memorizing class lists, developing mind association games, looking for cues in classrooms, reviewing each child's grade card, spending time looking at class pictures and seating charts, mentally reviewing names while observing in classrooms, and saying some over and over. Those who visit me frequently in the office, I come to know too well. Unfortunately, the well-behaved students, those who complete their work, follow the rules, and meet expectations, are those whose names I sometimes fail to learn.

People appreciate the effort it requires to know names. Visitors are always amazed by what they observe. I've learned to camouflage my weaknesses. Yet knowing names is always a priority and goal.

I have respect for colleagues in schools much larger than mine who are skilled at mastering so many more names. It is remarkable to observe them walk down a hallway, greet a child by name, ask a question about a sibling or an activity associated with the child or family. Usually, the child beams. It makes their day.

Principals have great influence in their schools. Knowing names of people in the school community is a critical skill in developing that influence.

Tip 10

Show Restraint

I've experienced angry, cursing parents, threats, and people who I thought were just plain crazy. Many throw temper tantrums, point their fingers, and eventually cry. When being publicly attacked, never respond. Others will be just as uncomfortable as you. It is better to allow them to counter on your behalf. What the principal says or does is always subject to public scrutiny. Stay calm. Realize that the person who is out of control and attacking you is doing so because he or she is afraid of something or feeling powerless. Many times, people attack the principal because of prior experience and frustration with others in positions of authority.

Don't make idle comments to others when you are in the hot seat. Attackers will assume you are talking about them and get angrier. Those who heard your comments will pass them along the gossip trail. Stay focused on issues. Don't let the attack become personal.

Board of Education meetings are infamous places for public tirades and displays of open hostility. Most of the time, reasonable people who are bystanders become very uncomfortable. Let others lose restraint. Hold your tongue. Be mindful of your body language, facial expressions, and eye contact. You as the principal set the tone and example for professional behavior.

There are times in the heat of the moment when the principal's voice must be heard. Focus on facts, take out any emotional tone in your voice, and be very brief. Very often, the best message is to take a ten-minute break.

Tip 11

Lead Regular Tours of the School

I enjoy giving visitors a tour of my school. Our superintendent enjoys visiting each classroom several times a year. Board members, community members, and new parents also enjoy the grand tour. There are so many positive things to see and observe, the kids are always special, and we proudly showcase one of the best-equipped and best-maintained facilities in the district.

If I'm unavailable, I delegate the role of tour guide to my secretary, volunteer coordinator, positive staff member, or even the leaders of the student council. Kids love giving tours of their school, and visitors tell me that their insights and comments are better appreciated, and more memorable, than those of adults.

When the superintendent walks with me, I try to give him information about each teacher and arm him with something unique he can say to an employee. There are always smiles and compliments, and people love the recognition that motivates them to do even more. Sometimes the compliments go both ways, making both the boss and me feel good.

For those who want to get ahead, plan these walk-throughs regularly—and don't tell anyone else about them!

Tip 12

Give Bonuses

But you say, "I work in school with negotiated salary schedules where I can't give monetary bonuses." Then, think of bonuses in other ways.

Give professional presentations—and take key staff members with you as participants (see Tip 98). Promoting careers and creating opportunities for others is perhaps more beneficial than any monetary reward, and it's more personal. People will appreciate the recognition of their professional abilities, and the time away at a professional conference can result in talk time, bonding, and reflection more valuable than any amount of money.

Allow flextime at work. Help those single moms or dads meet the schedule changes of babysitters. Enable people to avoid the rush hour traffic jams. Let people have some autonomy over their work. Allow a colleague engaged in graduate study some free time to study and complete pressing work.

Bonuses are not always in the form of money. Be creative. Find ways to reward people's accomplishments. It will be a bonus to your staff morale and school climate.

Tip 13

Become a Mastermind Thinker

Ever notice how some people seem to contemplate complex problems like a master chess player? They seem to visualize all the angles and potential moves? They rarely are blindsided or surprised. Effective principals are the same in their approach to analyzing complex situations. Their skill is particularly valuable in anticipating the human interests or political ramifications of issues facing their schools.

Effective principals add to their repertoire of considerations each time they face challenging decisions. They talk with each other. They share and reflect about how they worked through various considerations. They are not backward or intimidated. Rather, they open up and learn from others. They are constantly honing their thinking and problem-solving skills. They build on their experiences. They possess wide-angle vision but also clearly see how to move forward. They exemplify the old adage, "eyes and ears on all sides of their heads."

Personality and leadership tests identify mastermind thinkers. Skill development can be enhanced by reviewing the personal qualifiers that constitute these evaluations. Aspiring principals can acquire these abilities by closely observing effective mastermind thinkers, talking with them, and confiding with them as they face their own complex decisions.

Tip 14

Buy Time

Advocating this tip may pose some confusion or contradiction, especially since my dominant style is to be decisive and focused on task completion. But an effective principal knows when a decision must be made to move things along and when to buy time.

Some might describe those who buy time as procrastinators. But that is not the case. Procrastinators, for a variety of reasons, always tend to delay tasks or avoid making decisions. Effective principals intuitively realize when to move quickly, but they also know when to tread lightly, seek input, gain information, and make a better decision.

Late one Friday afternoon during my first principalship, a mother of an ornery kindergartner called to inform me that "Danny" had stolen her son's mittens on the bus. Danny was a developmentally delayed student with a history of behavior problems. I'd dealt with him numerous times. I'd also had interactions with the caller and been frustrated with her inability to handle her child.

My mistake was reacting to her complaints before buying time and getting all the facts. Knowing Danny's history, I called his parents. They questioned Danny, and they too assumed he was lying when he said he knew nothing about the mittens. They punished him during the weekend. I dread thinking what he might have endured.

Early the next Monday morning, the kindergarten teacher appeared at my office door asking if anyone had called about a pair of mittens she had found in her restroom. I knew immediately the owner, and I knew Danny was not a culprit.

Had I erred? Yes! Quickly trying to resolve before the week's end what I thought was a simple problem, I mistakenly fell for a parent's assumption, called Danny's parent, and hurt another child. I wish I had bought some time for Danny—and for me.

When I called the kindergartner's parent, I asked her to apologize to Danny and his parents. She reluctantly did. And we both learned valuable lessons. She was told to wait before calling the school with accusations of others—a mistake made too frequently by many parents. And I learned that a rush to be efficient is not always the most effective practice.

Take your time investigating problems with students, gain information, and learn from experience when to act and when to buy time.

Tip 15

Have a Security Plan in Place

Courageous principals remain calm and collected during a crisis because they have planned and practiced for emergencies. They've consulted with local emergency relief agencies, reviewed and updated plans and evacuation procedures, and taught people how to react in different situations.

Each school campus has unique considerations that will impact the evacuation and management process. It is best to have consultation and advice from officials who will be assisting in the event of an emergency. Document the meetings with these officials, especially their advice. Invite them to critique your emergency drills. Let the children and staff know who these people are, why they are visiting the school, what they should know and do in an emergency, and what you expect of their response and behavior. This is serious business that principals cannot take lightly. There have been enough incidents that one is foolish to assume a crisis cannot happen to them.

The principal's worst fear is that something will happen while he or she is out of the building. This worry impacts far too many principals' choices not to attend professional development opportunities, further isolating and adding to their stress. Develop back-up plans and don't sit around waiting for something bad to happen. No one benefits when leaders are afraid.

Tip 16

Memorize the Negotiated Agreements

The negotiated agreements between the Board of Education and certified and classified employees are your guides. Use them. Memorize them. Know the implications of every single line. Know it better than your subordinates do. From time to time, they may try to bully you and interpret the agreement to gain a particular advantage. Your comprehensive knowledge will help you avoid appearing negligent or weak.

Awareness and insights regarding the fine print and interpretations of the agreements will also keep you out of trouble. This lesson I have learned the hard way! Negotiated agreements are legal and must be followed. There is no excuse for doing otherwise. They provide the direction and spell out the responsibilities for the work of the school staff.

Not every issue can be anticipated and addressed in an agreement, of course, and from time to time people will challenge your decisions. Expect it. Don't react inappropriately. Follow the procedures, consider all points of view, and respond to grievances or questions in a professional manner. The negotiated agreements provide direction and define expectations for both the bargaining unit members and the administration. Know what the agreement expects of you as well as others.

Tip 17

Never Try to Conceal Big Problems

It's inevitable. Something will happen. The principal will sometimes be the last to know but will be held responsible. The media will soon be waiting outside the door. Like others who find themselves in tough situations, you may be tempted to "hide the elephant" or "sweep a problem under the rug." Remember Watergate? The Iran-Contra Affair? Monica Lewinsky?

It pays to tell the truth, accept the fallout, and move on. Hiding facts and information, assuming people will not find out, or hoping the problem will go away usually leads to bigger problems later. It is much harder to control rumors and put out fires than it is to tell the truth. It may be more tempting to hide, but in the long run, it is better to be open. Lies or misinformation lead to more lies and misinformation. Frequently, the way a situation is handled creates a bigger problem than the original concern. Turn on a stream of information.

Talk with practicing principals. They'll have their own personal examples of pitfalls and elephants they've wanted to hide. When you suspect you are on a precipice dealing with your own, call your trusted mentor and develop strategies that will enable you to move on, with support, rather than being engulfed in turmoil.

Tip 18

Never Shoot the Messenger

I'm fortunate to have people in my life who are critical friends. They tell me all sorts of things, but most important, when my ego or wings spread too far, they aren't afraid to correct me. From them, I hear the good and the bad. Because I love and trust them, I don't get angry when their message is something I don't want to hear.

Most people, however, display anger toward a person who is critical and delivers bad news. I've done it too often. But it is from those messengers that we receive critical information and insights. If we are smart, we'll seize the opportunity to learn and grow. Don't cast blame on them. They are being brave and helpful.

Listen. Show restraint if the message is not pleasant. Others are always watching. People will learn quickly to avoid you and uncomfortable situations if they feel they will be subject to tirades for telling you things you don't want to hear.

Who are the trusted messengers I've shot? There are many: my secretary, managing custodian and cook, union representatives, trusted teachers, colleagues, my wife, and family members.

Take a deep breath. Suck in your pride. Consider the message. Thank the messenger.

2

Vision

Mankind owes to the child the best it has to give.

—United Nations Declaration

Tip 19

Establish High Expectations

"Effective principals set high expectations and standards for the academic and social development of all students and the performance of adults" (NAESP, 2001, *Leading Learning Communities: Standards for What Principals Should Know and Be Able To Do,* p. 19). This requires principals to rethink what happens in their schools, why, and how things are done. There has always been great truth in the self-fulfilling prophecy. If principals don't have high expectations, they can't expect much of others.

For years, many have maintained a lower set of learning expectations for special needs students than regular students. Some special students were denied entry to the mainstream of the general curriculum because it was assumed to be too challenging. The amended Individuals With Disabilities Act in Education (IDEA) of 1997 addresses that misconception and clearly directs educators to enable all students appropriate access to the general curriculum. Principals must develop school cultures that are flexible and encourage collaborative, innovative, and supportive efforts to improve instruction for all students. Changing attitudes and years of practice can be challenging. But it must be done. It is the law.

Practicing principals can tell stories of variances in student achievement because of differences in expectations among teachers. I've known students who misbehaved or underachieved one year to suddenly become good students the next. It's all about expectations.

Effective principals articulate a clear vision about what they expect of adults and students. They do this more than once at the beginning of the year. They spend time explaining to students what they expect in achievement, behavior, attitude, and effort. They don't make excuses. They make sure learners have what they need to meet high expectations. They motivate, inspire, provide direction, and celebrate excellence.

Watch the successful NCAA collegiate football coaches on Saturdays. They exemplify high expectations. They expect their players to win. You would never assume they expect their teams to lose. Principals should take note and learn a lesson or two from these powerhouses.

Tip 20

Develop Effective, Challenging Goals

Principals are required to evaluate their staffs, and likewise, their performances should be evaluated. In addition to the typical checklist appraisal form, many negotiated agreements allow evaluations to be goal based. Principals sometimes complain about the minimal expectations of many of the goals they review. And then some turn around and write the same type of goals for themselves.

Coaches and players know their foremost goal is to score points and win games. They develop carefully planned strategies to accomplish their goals. Pianists know that to earn the gold cup in competition, they must practice daily. There is a goal and a vision of what things will be like when dreams are realized.

To select challenging goals implies some risk of failure. This scares many people. Ask any basketball player or golfer if they always score the big shots. They'll tell you they miss many more than they make. But they continue to practice. They learn by making mistakes and failing. They improve a little at a time. They have dreams of hitting it big.

Develop both professional and personal goals. Write them down. Goals should be classified by day, week, month, year, and multiyear. Know where you want to go and how you'll work to get there. Share your goals, and how you plan to achieve them, with your colleagues and friends. It doesn't help to keep your goals a secret. Others will never know if they can celebrate with you, and they can't help if they don't know your goals.

Principals must establish high expectations in their schools. You can model high expectations by selecting challenging goals, informing others of your dreams, and keeping people posted as to your progress. Modeling the process of setting a high standard, planning the steps to its achievement, and regularly assessing growth is one of the best lessons you can teach the students in your school.

Tip 21

Know the Trends in Education

Beyond the funding crisis in U.S. public schools and the No Child Left Behind Act, Gary Marx, in his book, *Ten Trends: Educating Children for a Profoundly Different Future* (2000, Educational Research Service, Arlington, VA), identified trends and challenges that affect educating children in the future. These are summarized as follows:

1. For the first time in history, the old will outnumber the young.

2. The United States will become a nation of minorities.

3. Social and intellectual capital will become the primary values in society.

4. Education will shift from averages to individuals.

5. The Millennial Generation will insist on solutions to accumulated problems and injustices.

6. Continuous improvement and collaboration will replace quick fixes and defense of the status quo.

7. Technology will increase the speed of communication and the pace of advancement or decline.

8. Knowledge creation and breakthrough thinking will stir a new era of enlightenment.

9. Scientific discoveries and societal realities will force difficult ethical choices.
10. Competition will increase as industries and professions intensify their efforts to attract and keep talented people.

These trends look ahead to the world our children will populate and lead. Educators also need to keep their fingers on the pulse of everything that effects the education of the children in their buildings and in our country right now. Among the trends and concerns on my current watch list that present both hope and challenge for myself and my fellow principals are these:

- Competition to find and keep talented employees
- Shortages in school leadership that make it incumbent on principals to develop professionals for leadership succession
- Impatient lawmakers who offer alternatives such as vouchers, tuition tax credits, and privatization of public schools
- Collaboration of educators in ways never experienced before
- Need for more functionally multilingual preparation for our youth who will be expected to work within a global business society
- The challenge of implementing the No Child Left Behind Act and IDEA (Individuals with Disabilities Education Act) without the promised funding, posing critical choices in regards to stretched budgets to achieve success and eliminate injustices for everyone
- Aging school facilities where maintenance or replacement are major concerns and big money issues in tough economic times
- Expansion of afterschool programming
- Improved communication and data management tools that promise to continue to rapidly change the way education does business

- Safety and security of schools, a major concern for school officials throughout the United States
- The rising rate of child obesity in elementary grades, a trend that has already shown an increase of incidents of child Type II diabetes, high blood pressure, and other symptoms of poor health
- Need for new curriculum to prepare students for an ever-changing world and increasingly demanding workplace
- Responsibility to successfully assimilate children from all parts of the world into our schools

To educate all our children in the years ahead, to actually *leave no child behind,* Americans must find a way to invest in *all* its schools—particularly its *public schools.* The most pressing challenge for the leaders in this country's schools is finding the way to reaffirm and redefine the purpose of *public* education, all the while addressing the current trends and challenges as outlined. Where some critics argue that the system is broken and outdated, others disagree. Change is inevitable and can be good. Our nation has emerged as a world power, in large part due to a continuously changing and improving educational system that produces an educated, informed populace. Despite all the criticism, the American public education system remains the envy and model to emulate for many other countries.

Tip 22

Determine Your Fundamental Beliefs About Education

Recently, while helping a young aspiring principal prepare for an upcoming interview, I challenged him to expound upon his fundamental beliefs about public education and the principalship. After a moment's thought, he deflected the question back to me, asking, "With all your experience, what do *you* really believe?" I was taken aback and struggled at first to expound my philosophy for my young protégé. But after a little time reflecting, I realized that I believe the following:

1. Children come first. Too often, educators lose sight of why schools exist. It is important to find time to be with the kids of my school.

2. All kids can learn.

3. Poor kids can learn—their experiences and relationships are simply lagging behind their more affluent peers.

4. Parents are children's most important teachers, and often we don't listen to them enough or provide them sufficient assistance.

5. It is important to teach the whole child and nurture each child's unique strengths.

6. Elementary students should be instructed in a heterogeneous, inclusive setting—an appropriate one that reflects the hopes and desires of our democracy and promotes self-worth and quality.

7. The key to good discipline is to teach the child appropriate expectations and choices, keeping punishment as a consequence for making bad choices.

8. Principals must empower teachers and others to effectively deal with student management and discipline.

9. The arts are a critical part of every child's education. The arts should be required and learning opportunities increased across the nation at all grade levels. Where the arts are valued and thrive, schools are effective.

10. All children have the right to be educated in a safe environment.

11. All children deserve an adequate and equitable public education. Facilities and resources should be dramatically improved in many of our nation's schools.

12. High-stakes tests are here to stay and are not all bad, but they should not be the only measure of a child's performance. Using test scores to denigrate instead of showing improvement will only create low morale and continued poor performance. Effective principals use multiple sources of data as diagnostic tools to assess, identify, and apply instructional improvement. So should our lawmakers.

13. Principals must have high expectations and standards for the academic and social development of all students and adults.

14. I am responsible for my own learning.

15. One of my most important tasks as a principal is to seek out and hire the best possible staff and to keep them.

16. Successful learning hinges on the quality of the teacher and the interpersonal relationships developed with students.

17. Successful principals develop strong networks with their colleagues.

18. Structure and consistency are important characteristics for teachers as well as principals.

19. Principals are responsible for community engagement and public relations of their schools.

20. Principals must create a shared responsibility for student and school success—delegation and sharing responsibility is critical to getting the job done.

21. Principals must have the necessary autonomy to be effective in their roles as instructional leaders.

22. Instructional leadership is the key aspect of the principalship, yet management tasks must still be a priority for good school operation.

23. Restructuring the principalship will enable leaders to be more effective and responsive to the needs of the school community.

24. Principals must have vision, plans, and strategies to achieve goals.

25. Principals need to *dress first class, think first class, and act first class.*

26. Every effective principal will at some time have to stand strongly for the right to challenge the system.

27. Protectionist union leaders all too often get in the way of significant improvement.

28. Leadership can be dangerous.

29. The principal sets the tone for the culture and everything that happens in the school.

30. Being a principal is the best job in the world.

Your list may not be this long. Bottom line: You need to determine those beliefs for which you will stand your ground, even sacrifice your job if necessary. Then, pick all other battles carefully. Strategize. Consult with your mentor. Don't burn bridges. Consider all sides of an issue, and make sure any battles you do take on are focused on issues, not other people.

Tip 23

Take Risks and Learn From Mistakes

You'll hear some principals say, "It's sometimes easier to beg forgiveness than it is to get permission." Comments such as these come from principals who are frustrated with bureaucracy and red tape. To move around numerous blocks, they choose to take risks, make things happen, and answer questions later if problems arise.

Effective principals realize that things don't always work smoothly the first time. Concepts are not always perfect, and the implementation of ideas sometimes goes astray. They accept that mistakes will be made.

Effective principals know that to make the most gains over time, they must have a consistent plan. They implement a plan, do, study, act (PDSA, sometimes known by other titles)—a procedure for continuous improvement. For major initiatives, they have groups of constituents gather information, read, review research, and plan an action. Then they do it, or conduct a pilot test. After a predetermined set of time, they study the results. They step back, reflect, look at data, consider alternatives, tweak the plan, and then choose to act on the findings or perhaps scrap the idea altogether. They avoid stabbing in the dark and having others perceive them jumping on bandwagons of the newest fad ideas. With the PDSA model, people have a chance to participate in decision making and accept ownership of the results.

Other times, principals must make decisions alone. If others won't, effective principals know when and how to ask tough questions. Effective principals learn to check with their mentors, buy time when they can, consider their best options, and make decisions focused on what is best for kids.

You will not always be right. Accept that you will make mistakes. Leaders lead while others follow. Leaders make things happen while others wonder what happened. Focusing on what is best for kids is always solid ground.

TIP 24

Be Decisive and Take Action

How many times have you attended meetings where important issues or questions were discussed, only to be tabled, referred to committee, or dropped altogether? Remember the feelings of frustration? Active people quickly get turned off and resent going to meetings where similar experiences might recur. Are you bored and apathetic at others' meetings? Do people get bored attending your meetings? It could be that they are tired of investing time and energy discussing important issues, knowing too well the outcome will be unproductive. This tip might seem contrary to consensus decision making, but it is not. There are simply times when the principal must act quickly and decisively for the good of all.

I once observed a meeting of principals where various ongoing issues were being discussed. It didn't take long to spot the various cliques of status quo good old boys and good old girls. The issues appeared to have historical, sentimental meaning to several of the participants but not the majority. Once the issues were aired (for what was likely the fifth time) and all opinions heard, the leader failed to move the items and initiate any decisive action. I was frustrated, and I was only a visitor. How must those with vital interest have felt?

Leaders need to know when it is appropriate to move and when to tread lightly. It takes courage to initiate actions. Although consensus is desirable for many decisions, the effective principal senses when it is appropriate to take action and demonstrate decisiveness. Let people know where you stand.

Tip 25

Embrace Diversity

I am envious of the principals of schools where there are numerous languages spoken, a colorful array of people, and a richness of world cultures impacting the learning of everyone. My school is located in a predominately white area, and my students miss the opportunity to play with, respect, and accept people of different backgrounds. We aren't learning and living in the real world. We've missed experiencing U.S. diversity!

Our diversity enriches us all. It is a source of strength and pride. We've come a long way, but there is much work remaining to enable every person to feel accepted and enjoy equal opportunities. Principals have done much to help the children of the world grow and learn together.

However, along with respect and appreciation for diversity comes adversity. New challenges and new demands will be put on our schools by ever-increasing groups of people. New biases and issues will continue to emerge. The work will never stop.

Change is a natural part of learning and experiencing life. Principals who don't experience regular doses of adversity had better reevaluate whether they are doing anything effective.

The United States is home to people from all parts of the world. We come in all shapes and sizes. Along with our diversity come many inherent problems. That's what makes us unique, presents many challenges, and yet creates more opportunities for growth than anyplace else in the world.

TIP 26

Don't Ride Dead Horses

Jim Grant is an internationally renowned educator and popular author. Fellow educators regard him as one of America's most passionate advocates for children. He is the founder and executive director of Staff Development for Educators, one of the nation's leading providers of professional development training for K–8 educators. He is also the cofounder of the National Alliance of Looping and Multiage Educators.

Jim, along with associate Char Forsten, has published a short, humorous allegory about education titled *If You're Riding a Horse and It Dies, Get Off*. Get a copy. It illustrates the need for change in schools very clearly.

There are numerous "dead horses" in our schools—ideas and approaches that just don't work. Too many of them are also sacred cows. Effective principals do what leaders and creative thinkers do: They challenge the continuing practices of riding those dead horses. They politely dismiss the suggestions of well-intentioned people who want to sustain programs or initiatives that plainly do not work. With support of others, effective principals take a fresh look at problems and design new plans that make sense and achieve results.

Work to remove the dead horses from your school. And not only the ideas that no longer work. Identify people, especially teachers, who should be removed and for whatever reason have not been. As long as these individuals stay, they can potentially ruin a year's education for a classroom of children and drag your school downward.

3

Student Learning

What we want for your children ... we should want for their teachers; that schools be places of learning for both of them, and that such learning be suffused with excitement, engagement, passion, challenge, creativity, and joy.

—Andy Hargreaves

TIP 27

Never Underestimate the Importance of Instructional Leadership

Not that many years ago, principals were evaluated and deemed effective mostly by how well they managed their school. If the buses ran on time, books were ordered, bills were paid, and beans were served for lunch, people thought the principal was doing a good job. And of course, principals kept order, disciplined unruly kids, developed the master schedule, and made sure there was soap in the restrooms and that they didn't smell.

That principalship doesn't exist anymore!

Today, although principals are still held accountable for overseeing many managerial tasks, they also are responsible for instructional leadership. To ignore management responsibilities is foolish. If the building is cold or dirty, the buses don't run on time, or the schedules are not effective, instruction and learning can be seriously affected. Those who learn to delegate create time to focus on instructional leadership.

What is instructional leadership? In the 1990s, this question became a hot discussion item. But principals were confused. Many of the people telling them how to be instructional leaders hadn't been in a school in years. They had no credibility, and many had no clue about the reality of a principal's daily work.

Principals play a key role in helping teachers and students reach effective performance levels of instructional and learning standards. In 2001, NAESP published *Leading Learning Communities: Standards for What Principals Should Know and Be Able To Do*. This best-selling document clarifies instructional leadership, and the standards were developed by principals for principals—just as doctors establish standards for their professional work. Principals from across the nation contributed to what constituted a definition of instructional leadership. The book is an excellent tool for new and veteran principals to use for reflection and self-evaluation. As outlined in the six standards, effective leaders

- Lead schools in a way that places student and adult learning at the center
- Set high expectations and standards for the academic and social development of all students and the performance of adults
- Demand content and instruction that ensure student achievement of agreed-on academic standards
- Create a culture of continuous learning for adults tied to student learning and other school goals
- Use multiple sources of data as diagnostic tools to assess, identify, and apply instructional improvement
- Actively engage the community to create shared responsibility for student and school success

While empowering teachers to participate in the decision-making processes related to what is taught and how, principals must be viewed as guides and coaches, leaders who establish high expectations and common direction. Effective instructional leaders regularly observe in all classrooms, guide lesson planning, create common planning time, monitor student learning, collect data, and use results to influence improvement plans. They expect daily evidence that teachers are providing quality instruction, but more than that, they ensure that all students are learning.

Effective principals do not allow managerial tasks to consume their days. They create adequate time to focus on being the instructional leaders of their schools. It is the key part of their job.

Tip 28

Understand the Child of Poverty

Poor kids can learn! You better believe that—but some principals don't. Yes, there are correlations between low socioeconomic status and low test scores. But that doesn't mean poor kids can't learn. They've just lacked experience. Some principals make excuses for their students' poor test scores and unruly behavior, citing the high poverty rate in their schools. Those principals are wrong!

Read *A Framework for Understanding Poverty* by Dr. Ruby K. Payne. She is an authority on this issue, and her books are a must read for anyone who works with children of poverty. As Payne explains, poverty does not always equate to a lack of financial resources. Nor is poverty always generational or a condition of single-parent families. Through case studies, Payne explains how those in poverty live, talk, and perceive the world. She describes the hidden rules of poverty, middle class, and wealth. The implications regarding building relationships, instruction, language development, and improving achievement provide excellent insights for school officials, especially principals. Read this book. Attend her professional workshops.

Poor kids shouldn't be scolded for not knowing something, nor should they be excused. They differ from middle-class peers in that they have not had the same experiences. Since schools and the business world operate from middle-class norms, principals must help everyone understand the hidden rules of the middle class, teach these rules, and help students and their parents become successful in the school setting.

Payne defines poverty as "the extent to which an individual does without resources." Likewise, schools are considered poor when they do without resources. Principals must become strong advocates for the resources they need. Use your voice. Speak up. Collaborate. Write about your experiences. Visit lawmakers. Don't make excuses. Don't stand by while middle-class and wealthy schools benefit from resources that those less fortunate deserve as well. This is a historic problem for our nation's schools. Principals must work steadfastly to get it fixed.

There are numerous shining examples of schools located in blighted areas where poor kids achieve at levels equal to or above more advantaged peers. It can be done. People in those schools just have to believe it can.

The principal sets the tone.

TIP 29

Be a Curriculum Leader

Principals who know how to write curriculum are in the best position to evaluate it and ensure that teachers understand it.

Effective school districts review and rewrite their curricula on a multiyear cycle. Typically, the review process involves input and participation from teams of teachers, parents, community members, and other constituents. Principals must be active participants and lead this process.

Principals must know the curriculum of all subject areas. They must know all areas, support all areas, and understand the diverse curricula of their schools. They are the guarantors that the curriculum provides the best possible foundation for instructing children in what they must know and be able to do.

Tip 30

Make Morning Announcements

I love morning time at my school. People are fresh, bright, and eager to learn and work. Immediately after the tardy bell rings, we begin morning announcements over the public address system. Fifth grade students look forward to the opportunity to help with the announcements and be that day's "voice of the school." We announce the lunch menu, guest teachers, and other information of interest to staff and students. We conclude with the Pledge of Allegiance and sing a patriotic song. An individual or small group (sometimes an entire class) is always recognized for displaying good citizenship and adhering to the code of conduct by leading the pledge and song. Parents have frequently videotaped this routine. It is my special time to see students in a positive way.

I always take part of this five-minute routine to reflect, teach, and clarify my expectations for students and adults. It is important that people hear my voice, that I set the tone for learning and provide structure to each day.

We keep this announcement time as short as possible. To some, it becomes routine. But most kids benefit from structure and routine. Each day begins smoothly with a positive feel, and I have a regular communication opportunity with everyone.

Structure is missing in schools where colleagues make announcements "when they get around to it." If all teachers began instruction when they got around to it or they felt like it, student achievement results would probably be low. Expectations are lower, lack of organization and planning is evident, and interruptions more frequent.

I observed effective morning announcements from my mentors and other principals with whom I worked. Making morning announcements forces me to adhere to a clock, review upcoming events, plan ahead, and act and sound positive.

The principal sets the tone. I expect the same dependability from the staff.

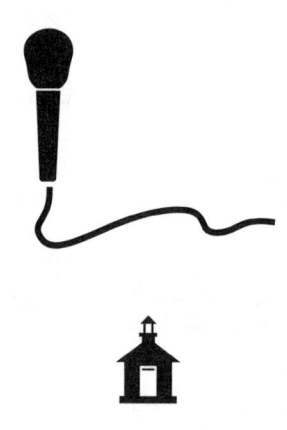

TIP 31

Eat Lunch With the Students

I try to stagger my dining experiences to cover all our lunch periods, and I learn so much from engaging the kids in conversation. The cooks, custodians, and cafeteria monitors tell me my presence improves student management. It also provides a relaxed opportunity for them to speak with me, as well as other staff members who pass by my special seat.

I've developed close relationships with some of my special needs students this way. While we enjoyed lunches together, one young girl, one of my favorite special students, learned how to hold her fork and engage others in conversation. And I was sending a clear message of acceptance and inclusion among all the students. She always brightened my most troublesome days. We both used our lunchtimes to help each other.

Eat lunch with the kids. They say the darndest things and will affirm every reason you identified for becoming a principal.

Tip 32

Support the Arts

The best schools have the best arts programs. Looking to improve your school's performance? Beef up the arts programs.

With ever-tightening budgets, a skewed obsession with test scores, and a fear of being labeled as a failing school, some principals are creating more instructional time in the three R's by reducing or eliminating students' time in the arts. They say they are preparing students to meet state and national standards, pass tests, and become competitive as adults within a fast-changing global economy. But they may be depriving their students the opportunities that will best help them become creative thinkers—perhaps the most important characteristic for a competitive edge for their future.

What is a good, adequate education? One that leads to a good job? Certainly, we want every child to read, write, and compute. But we also must make sure students can develop human values, such as the ability to get along with others, respect human life, maintain integrity, and be fair and just. The arts affect the mind and spirit. They open eyes, ears, and feelings.

The arts help everyone define who they are, broaden perspectives, expand abilities to express themselves and communicate, develop imagination, make judgments, and escape the mundane. The arts help people learn to feel and care. They help us learn to be empathetic. We cannot allow our children to be cheated of these critical abilities that shape their personal development. Understanding the arts helps people appreciate some of the highest historical achievements and wisdom of human beings. Without them, people are less well educated. There simply is no alternative or replacement.

The arts in elementary and middle level schools must be more than cute bulletin boards, cut-and-paste craft activities, and an occasional music program for parent meetings. Students must have exposure to the full gamut of arts activities: creative writing, dance, music, drama, and the visual arts. The arts must be more than a time filler for the contractual resource period of classroom teachers. They must be taught through an interdisciplinary approach with other subject matter. They will enhance learning across the entire curriculum.

I once worked for a superintendent who confessed that he hadn't had a creative thought in twenty years. He lacked a background in the arts. Enough said.

Tip 33

Support All Extracurricular Activities

Support everything in which your students participate. Attend their ball games. Encourage participation in computer, service, and science clubs. Support the band and 4-H clubs. Recognize the efforts of the chess club. Show that you care. Everyone needs an outlet and involvement in something. The goodwill that will come from providing your students with a variety of activities will be well worth the investment.

My experience has been that students who participate in activities outside the school day learn skills that they would never gain in the classroom setting. They develop a sense of belonging and learn how to be team players. They learn self-discipline. They learn to spend their leisure time wisely. Where students are fortunate to have parent support, extracurricular activities often help bring the family closer together. Extracurricular activities help stimulate motivation, setting of goals, and lasting friendships. They become a source of pride and identification for communities.

I challenge those parents who want to take away sports or activities for punishment because their child does poorly in school. I tell them they are taking away the child's opportunities for a positive identity, association with good role models, and enjoyment in their lives. There are many other alternatives. I won't sit by and watch this happen without raising issues. I refuse to allow them to limit their child's future because of their lack of interest or busy schedules. Parents choose to have children—they have a responsibility to make sure the whole child has opportunities to develop.

There are elementary and middle school principals who choose to downplay the importance of extracurricular activities. They prefer to let their secondary colleagues enjoy all the responsibility and involvement. But many high school activities require skill development at the elementary or middle levels. Students need the chance to explore, grow, find themselves, and make mistakes before their fragile identities are challenged as teenagers.

Get involved. Show your students you care. Ask questions about their involvement and participation. Encourage them. Know their coaches and club sponsors. Include recognition of students' accomplishments during your morning announcements. You and your students will reap the benefits.

Remember the old adage. "All work and no play will make Jack a dull boy." It's true!

Tip 34

Focus on Discipline by Teaching, Not Punishing

After just a few days on the job at my school, staff members told me about "code pink." They explained it was their signal and method of providing assistance to each other when students "went off." It didn't take me long to observe angry kids, frustrated adults, and a student management system in need of an overhaul. We quickly dispensed with code pink and set about creating a code of conduct that focused on instruction rather than rules, consequences, and punishments.

The Ohio Classroom Management Project provided our small team the guidelines and examples of best practices we needed. We learned from others. Slowly, our team presented alternatives to our staff, brought in teams to share, and arranged for visitations in other districts. It took months, but we adopted the following simple code of conduct using the best of everything we reviewed:

W—Work for Quality

E—Earn Respect

S—Safety First

T—Treat Others Kindly

When kids were caught violating a portion of the code of conduct, they were asked to explain their choice rather than being scolded. Teachers soon found that many students had no concept of right or wrong, didn't understand expectations, and had to be taught how to behave and get along with others in the school setting. Eventually, by focusing on what was good rather than bad, problems diminished, attitudes changed, and the management of students became much easier. Discipline means "to teach." Once kids were taught what they could and couldn't do, most conformed. It wasn't necessary to have code pinks because the behaviors became less threatening. Expectations of everyone were raised to levels previously thought impossible.

I don't like being corrected in public for something I don't know how to do or know nothing about. I'm well aware that it is illegal to exceed the speed limit in my car. When caught, I accept the punishment. But I might not know that it is wrong to run down a busy sidewalk. To be circled and chastised in front of others is insulting, and I'd likely rebel. Continual ridicule and punishment without understanding just makes me angrier.

Kids feel the same. Teach them what they need to know. Expect them to make mistakes. Our job is to prepare them to live successfully in the adult world. It is much better to always be teaching rather than spending valuable time punishing.

Tip 35

Determine How You'll Make Classroom Placements

As one academic year ends, principals begin planning for the next. Classroom assignments are commonly made in late May, before the end of the year.

Many years ago while I was completing an administrative internship, I observed classroom assignments as the principal's task. Input from parents was not sought. Parents were expected to accept whatever placement decisions were made.

Times have changed. Choice is becoming a more and more common part of the school culture. We advocate for parental involvement, and what better form of involvement is there than developing a high level of comfort and respect between parents and teachers as placements are made? When parents are permitted to make a wise, informed decision and request a teacher that will challenge and best meet the needs of their children, the potential for involvement and success is greatly improved.

I've given numerous presentations at state and national conferences on this topic. Principals across the country have developed myriad processes regarding their placement decisions. They do what works for their school. There appears to be a strong majority of principals who welcome parental input. They have safeguards, however. They monitor the balance of race, gender, ethnicity as well as academic and behavior potential and achievement of all students. They frown on parents who make requests because, "All of Susie's friends are in the other classroom!" It can be a rough year for a teacher if a parent doesn't want his or her child in a particular teacher's class. Don't ignore past history and experience. Gather as much information as you can. Include teachers in the decisions. They know each other's strengths and weaknesses and most often will work to create equity in class assignments.

Know what you want to do. Talk with colleagues in your district. Perhaps this decision-making process has district guidelines and policies. Whatever you determine, inform parents via newsletters, meetings, and your Web site of your policy and timelines for their input. Do what is best for the children. Doing so, you increase everyone's chance for happiness and success.

Tip 36

Learn What's Special About Special Education

I've learned a great deal about special education during the time I've been a principal. Early on, I was so inexperienced I didn't know what to question. But with time and training, I came to admire and appreciate the expertise of many "special educators" and the good things they did for kids. Yet because I've always wanted *every* child to succeed, I've been uncomfortable and struggled when I thought priorities or balance of services appeared out of kilter.

Special educators have helped me gain a broader appreciation for diversity and differences among all people. They've helped me understand how they can best fit the structure of our school and support the learning of all students. They've helped me understand and justify accommodations. I now understand how standards can be adapted for all learners. We are the same yet different. It is OK.

At my school, we have worked to remove labels and include all students in our learning environment. Special education has become an asset rather than a burden. Special educators team teach with regular education staff—everyone benefits, especially the students. We've gained access to resources and training we would otherwise not have had. We are more knowledgeable, better trained, and more responsive to all students' needs.

Learn everything you can about the Individuals with Disabilities Education Act (IDEA). Support the work of special education staff. Evaluate and adjust your attitudes in support of special education. Become a special principal.

Tip 37

Master Conflict Resolution Skills

Healthy resolution of conflicts needs to permeate every school's culture from top to bottom. The commitment needs to start with the principal and include all members of the learning community. Principal, students, teachers, and support staff need to share the process and the values.

Recognize that conflict can be good. Without some conflict, change is probably not happening in your school. Principals can't adequately perform their duties without saying "no" to someone, potentially causing a conflict situation. Conflicts of varied intensity will arise whenever competing interests surface—between students and other students, teachers and students, parents and teachers, and teachers and principals.

There are many excellent conflict management instructional programs. To effectively implement these programs, all adults, including the principal, must be trained. They must model the concepts and continually reinforce students' learning. Students can quickly internalize strategies for resolving their conflicts when they observe modeling by adults. Parent training helps institutionalize the modes of behavior taught at school and includes families of members in your learning community in a meaningful way.

Principals *must* have continual training in conflict resolution. They must know their personal inclinations in dealing with conflict. Conflict is inevitable. Learning to deal with conflict by effectively focusing on the issues while avoiding being consumed emotionally is a critical skill.

Tip 38

Visit Three Classrooms Each Day

Visit three classrooms each day. This goal was established by my superintendent. For many reasons (feeling overwhelmed, time, managerial tasks, paperwork, etc.), I felt he'd struck a nerve when he made this announcement at a principals' meeting. I knew there were days when I had felt trapped in the office and hadn't even made it to the hallway, let alone a classroom.

I began documenting the classrooms I visited. Like teachers calling on students for responses in their classrooms, I discovered I frequented some classrooms more than others. Those classrooms where the teacher was difficult to like, I found myself visiting less frequently. Those I liked or respected more were enjoyable to visit. My data analysis helped me refocus and develop a plan that ensured I equitably visited all classrooms.

I learned all sorts of things. And some people began devoting more time on task when they thought I might be popping through the door. We were able to make some adjustments where needed. Classroom management, instruction, and learning improved. Visiting classrooms became comfortable and helped create a supportive, positive climate in the school.

Instructional leaders have no alternative. Make the time. Visit at least three classrooms. Make mental notes or record what you see. Positive experiences can become the subject of the three handwritten notes you will write after everyone else has gone home.

Tip 39

Take Pictures Regularly

Invest in a digital camera that can continually be available to you. Get a good one and learn to use it. They are easy and economical to use. Take pictures at every major school event as well as during typical school days. Document the learning and good things that happen in your school.

To use the pictures of children and adults for a variety of purposes, follow district confidentiality guidelines and safeguards regarding publishing photographs. If your school district doesn't have a policy, consult your state association for advice and guidance.

Create PowerPoint™ presentations for staff meetings, inservice sessions, parent meetings, community gatherings, and professional conferences where you may be invited to speak. Along with the digital camera, invest in the projectors and accessories needed to produce quality presentations. Send photos to accompany articles in newspapers, include them in your parent newsletters, and post copies throughout the school. Regularly post pictures on your school's Web site. Taking pictures is a practice that will enable you to capture the year and document quality work and learning in your school.

People love to hear stories. If they can't hear you, let them read about and see your school through written stories with pictures.

Pictures are worth a thousand words. Tell the good word about your school.

Tip 40

Organize a Student Council

Allow students an opportunity to voice their opinions about their school. Even young students can learn how to share their thoughts about school governance and improvement with proper, patient assistance. You might be surprised what you'll learn if you provide students with a nonthreatening atmosphere to share their opinions.

Visit the Student Services section of the NAESP web site (http://www.naesp.org/kids.html) for a variety of resources available to assist with establishing a student council. Many state associations sponsor training workshops for students, their advisors, and principals.

Select a good advisor or advisors. It is usually best if the individuals are staff members, though parents have also enjoyed success as advisors. In some schools, cooks and custodians have played key roles with student governance.

Encourage the student council to accept responsibilities beyond simply organizing special spirit days or fund raising. Meeting for the sake of meeting will get old fast. Enable participants to learn the basics of running effective meetings, speaking publicly, and representing the views of their classmates. Young students can learn parliamentary procedure. The skills they learn will enable them to become leaders throughout their lives. Make sure the student council is viewed with respect. Staff support and buy-in of the concept are important. Create a set of bylaws. Expect students to understand the responsibilities and expectations of representing themselves and their school. The principal must never neglect responsibility for what the student council does.

4

Adult Learning

The art of choosing men is not nearly so difficult as the art of enabling those one has chosen to attain their full worth.

—Napoleon

Principals, leading by example, should identify professional development opportunities to improve their own craft.

—NAESP
(2001; *Leading Learning Communities: Standards for What Principals Should Know and Be Able to Do*)

Tip 41

Hire Good People and Invest in Them to Keep Them

When a teaching position opens at my school, I view it as an opportunity to strengthen the staff and improve our overall performance. I fight for the right to interview as many viable candidates as I can. I consider what the students of the vacated classroom need, the type of person the staff would like to work with, and the strengths and weaknesses of the existing staff. I try to find a candidate who can fill a special need. Résumés, transcripts, and references don't always indicate a strong teacher. I look for the diamond in the rough.

Don't get me wrong. Do take time to review credentials—thoroughly. Once you have narrowed potential candidates for consideration, check references. Since only a fool would list a reference that would say something bad, use your vast network of professional contacts to find out the real story about a candidate. Do thorough work. Select a candidate who is coachable and has a desire to grow. Once you hire a person, build a rapport that will enable the beginning teacher to learn from mistakes within a safety net. Reduce fear. Help the newly assigned veteran to your school quickly adjust to working and contributing among new colleagues.

Leaders throughout history have been successful when they have surrounded themselves with good people. Often, leaders take a back seat and allow those on the frontlines to shine. Leaders take great pride in the teams they have put together, and they devote time and energy to developing their fullest potential.

Teacher shortages make hiring good people even more challenging. There are fewer good people to go around. Keep a focus on the important task, set high expectations for yourself and others, and good people will find their way to your school. They will want to be part of a winning team.

Once you've hired the best people, spend your resources helping them get even better. You want to keep good people once you've found them. Train and reward them. Establish an expectation that teachers and support staff regularly attend state and national conferences and workshops and seminars that relate to their assignments or professional growth plans. Find the necessary resources to pay their expenses and make the experience memorable. Expect people to give presentations. Model the same yourself. Share the good things that happen at your school. Participating with your staff during inservice training can be a wise investment of your time for bonding and team building. Don't be afraid to leave the school to learn as a group.

Whereas business managers might be able to invest in their brightest by offering higher salaries or bonuses, principals, without the freedom of merit pay, can't vary compensation differently than the negotiated salary schedule. But they can offer other rewards. All people appreciate emotional benefits, such as praise, trust, independence, freedom, respect, and flexibility to do their jobs.

Encourage your staff to establish personal and professional goals as part of the staff development plan. Help find the resources to realize the goals. People will appreciate the investment in their learning and future.

School district officials who insist on hiring candidates at the bottom of the salary schedule are foolishly moving toward mediocrity. Not that beginners can't be developed into superstars, but it is safer to invest in master teachers with a proven record who can bring new ideas and best practices and model them for the existing staff. The superstars can provide some of the best staff development possible. Challenge the thinking and practices of your boss if you find yourself in a district where the prevailing thought is to hire the most inexperienced, lowest-paid teacher. Look elsewhere yourself if you can't change that thinking.

Tip 42

Staff Development Must Be Ongoing

When I became principal of West School, one of the first decisions I faced was whether to continue using the services of a California-based language arts consultant with whom my staff and predecessor had begun working. I'd heard about Dr. Kay Brallier, but we hadn't met until after my assignment was confirmed.

She was highly recommended by Dr. Maria Wilkes, the district curriculum supervisor. She cautioned that I'd make a mistake if I didn't get behind the integrated language arts initiative already begun. She said it was a learning process that would take time, and I would be wise to learn all I could.

I did, and it's transformed a low-achieving school into one of continuous progress and growth. The positive change couldn't have occurred without the support of an expert and the patience of Kay Brallier. My role was to find the resources through grants to ensure her continued involvement with my staff. It wasn't always easy. The best consultants command hundreds of dollars per day. I wanted the best for my staff. And when the heat was on and change became difficult for some, I ran interference with district politics when the temptation grew to look elsewhere for consultant support.

That's been part of the historical problem in my district and numerous others with staff development. Change takes time. Getting teachers to change attitudes and revamp their planning and methodology takes time. It can't be accomplished with a one-time on-site visit, seminar, or workshop.

And much too often, as change takes place, when the heat gets turned up during the storming process, staff development consultants get the boot. I've watched too many district consultants come and go. Many times and in many places, teachers are told to try this and then that. There isn't a consistent focus or plan. No wonder teachers become cynical and say, "Don't worry, this too shall pass!"

Consultants are also at risk when a change in administration takes place. I hadn't given that any consideration during that first meeting with Kay. She had to decide whether or not to stay as well. She didn't have to work in my school. She had plenty of work in California. But she had developed a high level of respect and commitment with my teachers. Together, we agreed to forge a relationship and move to an even higher professional level.

Talk with other principals. They'll tell you how to find the best consultants. Build a strong relationship with the person you choose. Expect some heat when change takes place. Share your experience with others. Celebrate your successes over time.

Tip 43

Give Your Superstars What They Need and Let Them Fly

For years I worried and devoted my attention trying to help struggling students (and staff members) improve their performance. That all changed following a memorable "Ah ha" moment while attending a conference in Cleveland.

In college, like others, I learned about the bell curve and how in any sample population, approximately two thirds of the sample would be in the middle, with high and low achievers at varying standard deviations at either end of the curve. With our student populations, those at the low end of the curve are often placed in special education and those at the high end in gifted classes. Most often, special education resources and staff are more plentiful than those for the gifted. And the special education students (and their teachers) require inordinate amounts of time, attention, frustration, and sometimes legal battles—all too often without effecting significant, lasting changes.

At the Cleveland conference, the presenter challenged us to reflect on our teaching staffs. He said in every school, teachers could be classified into one of three groups: *superstars, backbones, and mediocres*. And when asked which group received the highest percentage of our time, most of us responded: *mediocres*. Teachers could view students in much the same way, and typically respond the same about their students.

Then the Ah-ha moment! As the presenter explained, I realized that it's the superstars who really hold the potential to transform our schools. I'd been allowing the wrong group to dominate my time. The superstars, when given permission, will fly on their own, make things happen, and by their extraordinary ability and effort, skew the backbones to even higher performance. And the mediocres—those staff members who complain and do only the minimum—probably won't ever change. Despite all my past efforts to help, they hadn't, so I decided to focus on the others. I put my thoughts into the form of an article such as this and shared it at a staff meeting. At that meeting and afterwards, I informed the staff that I wouldn't neglect the needs of the mediocres, but I refused to allow them to further dominate my time, the climate of our building, or the realization of our goals.

My school changed. The superstars, always eager for new challenges, were empowered to stretch their wings. I was thrilled to support the best our school had to offer, and the backbones soon began following the lead, no longer held back by the insecurities of the few.

Principals play the *key role* in school improvement, just as a quality teacher is the critical part of classroom success. Many administrators routinely devote resources and time for staff development, often with disappointing results. Who gets the most attention in typical staff development? The superstars? Doubtful.

Real school reform will happen when we release the superstars from the constraints we've inadvertently put on them. Give them what they need, and get out of their way. Quality results are sure to follow, and the bell curve will begin to change.

Tip 44

Don't Squash Others' Ideas

I hate it when people squash my ideas before giving them any consideration. People who say, "We've tried that before," "that's not in my job description," "I don't have time," or "that's just one more thing I have to do" frustrate me. They are negative, cynical, and think most about how ideas affect them rather than what might be good for children.

Try hard to listen and consider ideas of staff and parents without quickly casting the "it won't work" sentence on an idea that they've contemplated and shared. Nothing shuts down creativity and free-flowing ideas and perpetuates the status quo more than the squashing of a newly hatched idea. Students quickly withdraw and stop contributing to class discussions when they perceive their ideas are cast aside and not valued.

I have to be particularly careful during Intervention Assistance Team meetings not to squash my creative thinkers. There are times when team members, and sometimes parents, are too quick to kill suggested strategies. They say, "I've tried that before, and it won't work." But all good ideas need nurturing, freedom to develop, support over time, and encouragement from the boss. If you do the same things as you've always tried before, you'll get the same results. Encourage your free thinkers. Idea people are usually different. They frequently are right-brained thinkers. They are often not detail oriented.

It takes all kinds of people to make an effective school. Embrace rather than shoot down the idea people. You need them!

Tip 45

Learn How to Ask Questions

Many times when my daughters were teenagers, *how* I asked them questions was just as important as the question being asked. It had to do with the tone of my voice and the type of response I wanted to hear. If I casually asked what they did at school, they'd often blow me off like most kids and say, "Nothing!" Those are words a principal doesn't want to hear, so the cycle of our conversation usually turned downward. Like all teenagers, they were experiencing many emotions and exploring their limits, and mom and dad always seemed to be complaining and "coming down on them." I've learned since that asking "what good questions did you ask at school today (or what good things did you do)?" would have focused our conversations in a much better way.

Time and again I've noticed the same with teachers and parents. Because of perceived vagueness, when conducting an evaluation conference or a parent conference, it is sometimes tempting to be direct and tell the individual what you want them to do or what you see as a weakness in performance. But experience has shown that it's best to lead with questions such as "what do you think about this?" or "have you thought of trying this?" If I display appropriate body language, good eye contact, and a pleasant tone of voice, this line of questioning most often triggers a thoughtful response. If my questioning is too direct or has an insinuating ring, I can expect a defensive answer. When that happens, the conversation moves in a direction that I didn't want it to go.

Principals can control most conversations in which they are engaged. Learn how to ask questions that lead to positive responses. Teach others how to ask good questions. Engaging others in productive conversations is a skill that effective principals can model for others.

Tip 46

Avoid District Politics

Every organization has an informal gossip grapevine, sometimes called the "gripevine." It seems to be human nature. Principals are often the subjects of the gossip. And there are people who thrive making sure principals are told about the gossip, hoping to gain favor or perhaps just to fan the flames. While information is shared, good or bad, the principal's response is being watched. Sometimes, saying nothing, a look of the eye, or a smile causes the gossip to spread even more. That is why the principal must always be careful. It is safer, in most circumstances, to stay away from the grapevine and avoid being drawn into inappropriate discussions.

There is often some credibility to the information on the grapevine. It would be hard for someone to dream up all the things that are circulated. But it serves the principal no purpose to be closely aligned to this network, especially if the information tends to be negative and hurtful of others.

Sometimes, principals are promoted in districts where they taught. They have familiarity with the network and district politics. Temptation is always there, and it is challenging to forego a constant fix of news.

The principal also can't be oblivious. That would be foolish as well. Effective principals find the balance and maintain a professional distance from those who thrive on nothing more than gossip.

There are politics in every organization just as there is a grapevine. Schools exist in a public arena. Principals must always be aware of the politics around them. And as middle managers, it is best to be neutral.

Once the principal is observed providing political favors, making exceptions for influential people, or playing the game in a self-serving manner, it is hard to return to neutrality. People will lose trust, and others will seek to gain advantage. Yet there are times when principals will have to take a stand. It is safest to fight for issues, keeping personalities at bay. Not everyone will understand, but at least the principal will be viewed as consistent.

Principals cannot be apolitical. But don't be trapped and become consumed by district politics. Too many jobs have been lost by those who thought otherwise.

Tip 47

Run Effective Meetings

No one likes it when scheduled monthly district administrative meetings are delayed for late arrivers. Make it a point to arrive at meetings and events on time. Certainly, emergencies will occur, and a courtesy phone call lets others move ahead as planned. Over time, it seems the same people are always on time or late.

Teachers have terrific demands on them. Nothing frustrates them more than a principal late to a meeting. This should be the exception rather than the rule. Start meetings on time and expect all staff to be present and prepared to work.

A good deal of a principal's time is spent in meetings with a variety of constituents. Principals should have training in how to conduct efficient meetings, how to establish norms of expected behavior, and how to manage time and meeting outcomes. Each meeting should be approached with a vision of desired outcomes and with consideration of the time of those attending. The principal's demeanor sets the tone for all the outcomes. If you are humorless, don't expect laughter. If you frown, you'll see frowns. If you snap at people, expect them to snap back. If you show restraint dealing with challenges, others will do the same and support you when mistreated. Preparation and demeanor are keys to good meetings.

Prepare an agenda and distribute it in advance. List those who should attend the meeting. Set starting and ending times.

Establish group norms. Delineate responsibilities, set discussion time limits, and list expected outcomes. List how and when decisions will need to be made. Develop follow-up plans when necessary. Share facilitation opportunities. Have a timekeeper and a note taker. Evaluate meetings from time to time for effectiveness.

Don't have a meeting unless there is a good reason to have one. Meeting for the sake of meeting hardly ever produces anything useful.

Tip 48

Keep the Monkeys on the Backs of Others

There are days when it seems like I'm working in a zoo. I sometimes feel overwhelmed by all the problems that come to the office, especially on days when the everyone acts like monkeys out of their cages.

Recently, while waiting for a flight to Columbus from Rochester, New York, I purchased and read Blanchard, Oncken, and Burrow's *The One Minute Manager Meets the Monkey*. In less than an hour, my dilemma was described, and I was filled with ideas of how productivity within the school setting could be improved.

The authors described *monkeys* as "problems on the backs of people." As students and adults revolve through my office, they have their monkeys solidly on their backs. And it seems everyone wants to be free of these burdens, and they try to place them squarely on my back. Often I feel as though I am completely bent over by the weight of monkeys!

The book reminded me of sage advice from my first superintendent (who also must have known this story). He said, "When people leave your office, make sure they always keep their monkeys on their backs." I should have better contemplated his advice. What was he talking about—monkeys?

As I read on, I realized my feelings of frustration were highest on days when I filled my office with monkeys. Sometimes there appeared to be monkeys everywhere—the lights, files, desk drawers, in the phone. Nothing I did seemed to get any of them to leave the office. These days were becoming commonplace, and colleagues shared the same scenarios in their offices.

By keeping other people's monkeys in my office, I was sending the message that I *wanted* their monkeys. I often gathered so many monkeys I couldn't attend to my own. And when others' monkeys were in my office, my staff and students were denied the opportunity to care for and feed them. When I procrastinated and failed to return monkeys to their owners, everything in the school seemed to stall. No one seemed to attend to the needs of the monkeys, and they were often out of their cages. Chaos and gridlock would be good descriptors.

Then, I read these profound words: "All monkeys must be handled at the lowest organizational level consistent with their welfare!" (p. 68). And I suddenly understood my first superintendent's advice. Most often, people know best how to care for their own monkeys. My task was to make sure people always left the office keeping their monkeys on their own backs. It is clear that some monkeys have to remain with the principal, but most should leave with their owners and be cared for at a lower organizational level, like teachers or students.

Most monkeys seem to be related to student discipline and management. Principals and teachers spend much of their time in dialogue about these monkeys. Monkey management, and the overall operation of schools, will improve when school personnel follow these guidelines:

1. The dialogue between a principal and a teacher (or student) should not end until the monkey has been completely described.

2. The monkey's ownership must be assigned to a person.

3. Once the monkey is described and its ownership determined, the next moves for dealing with the monkey must be specified.

4. Teachers (as well as students) need assurance that addresses the risk of dealing with the unpredictable moves of monkeys. The principal can give assurance simply by directing the teacher to provide a recommendation followed by an action, or, when there is more confidence with the situation, instructing others to take action with an eventual report about outcomes.

5. And last, principals must allow time for monkeys to be fed and cared for by others. And there must be time established for regular checkups.

It all seemed so simple. The authors' rules for monkey management were summarized (p. 94) as follows:

1. Describe the monkey.

2. Assign the monkey.

3. Ensure the monkey.

4. Check on the monkey.

Success with these rules leads to delegation. By delegating the management of monkeys, teachers become empowered to deal with their own monkeys (most often students). They become more confident and self-reliant and experience less stress. They learn to move monkeys to lower levels of the organizational structure.

When monkeys are well managed, fed, *and cared for in their own cages,* the productivity of the school is dramatically increased.

Tip 49

Encourage Consensus Decision Making

Principals conduct and facilitate numerous meetings and attend many other meetings where someone else is in charge. Meeting effectiveness can be enhanced when there is active participation, and people appreciate being able to shape decisions that affect them. When decisions are made that require buy-in from others, consensus is the best way to go. Consensus is usually not everyone's first choice, but it's a type of decision everyone can live with. If someone can't live with it, it's up to him or her to make a counterproposal.

Consensus does *not* mean . . .

- A unanimous vote
- Everyone's first choice
- That everyone agrees, although enough need to be in favor to get the decision carried out

To be sure, consensus decision making takes more time, energy, and training. Most groups find that energy spent on front-end discussion results in a far more efficient and effective implementation of the decision later on. On the other hand, quick "down and dirty" voting often results in very poor implementation. Spend the energy up front, or spend even more energy later!

Good consensus decisions mean that . . .

- All participants contributed resources
- Participants accepted the use of one another's resources and opinions
- Participants viewed "different" as helpful rather than as a hindrance
- Everyone can paraphrase the issue
- Everyone has a chance to describe his or her feelings about the issue
- Those who continue to disagree indicate publicly that they are willing to go along for an experimental try for a prescribed period of time
- All share in the final decision

If consensus cannot be reached, a group can always fall back on some win-lose method, such as voting, or executive decision. However, it is very difficult, if not impossible, to move from a win-lose approach to a more collaborative, win-win style.

Like most administrators, my big question is, "How can I involve my learning community in decision making without giving up my ultimate responsibility and accountability for the final decision?"

The key to this problem lies in the definition of consensus. Remember, consensus is reached when everyone in the group can live with the decision without feeling compromised. As a member of the group, the principal's approval is necessary for consensus. Your veto blocks consensus. Since voting is not permitted, you can't be outvoted by your subordinates. The group must develop a solution that you can support wholeheartedly. If consensus is impossible, then the decision is placed back in your hands and you can exercise your right to make an executive decision.

No one likes a dictator. Generals are needed in the military to oversee a hierarchy of strict command necessary for battle. Schools don't operate like the military or the penal systems, but some principals earn reputations like leaders from those worlds.

Good principals are sensitive to the needs of others and know when and how to move things along. The bottom line is that the buck stops with you, and you'll have to know when to make certain decisions. Just remember that consensus is best in the long run.

5

Data

Failure is success if we learn from it.

—Malcolm Forbes

Tip 50

Collect, Manage, Analyze, and Use Data to Drive Decisions

In a world of accountability, principals must be the leaders in collecting and analyzing data to shape decisions that lead to continuous improvement. But the models of best practice of this standard of what principals should know and be able to do remain few.

What kind of data? How are they analyzed? How does a principal use them?

It's more than just test scores. Data should be both quantitative and qualitative. Principals must encourage others to collect a variety of data while always being on the search for information about their students and school performance. The most reliable qualitative data will likely come from other sources. People often soften their remarks and feedback when speaking to the principal because of the position of authority.

Read Rudy Giuliani's autobiography, *Leadership,* and see the parallels of how he identified problems and developed data collection and tracking systems to lower New York City's crime statistics. Study Malcolm Gladwell's book, *The Tipping Point,* to gain an understanding of how the little things can make a profound difference in societal change. The insights will enable you to better focus on the kinds of data that must be collected as well as the manner in which the data should be analyzed before new actions are planned.

Talk with people and listen to what they say. Review grade cards, attendance and tardiness records, code of conduct infractions, and suspension records. Assess your students' problem-solving skills; higher-order reading, writing, and thinking skills; and school climate and morale. Collect data regarding students' socioeconomic status, number of computers, and books in the library. Compare data of student ability at the start of school with progress at the year's end. Look for trends. Look for gaps. Study other schools. Set high expectations. Make no excuses.

Tip 51

Use Tests for Diagnostic Purposes

There is danger in using the results of state and national tests to compare schools. Tests should be used for diagnostic purposes. Educators need to establish a baseline of students' abilities and then use tests to gather information that will help guide instruction, leading to a measure of individual growth and learning at a predetermined time. The high stakes and pressure that is impacting our young children and educators will not achieve long-lasting school reform and mastery of critical-thinking skills.

Learning must be fun. We have to guard against letting high-stakes tests rob our youth of the enjoyment of learning.

It is unlikely that high-stakes testing will go away. So principals must use their voices and better educate the public about tests. This information must be simple and easy to understand, factual, relevant, and meaningful to the audiences. There need not be any excuses; let the facts speak for themselves. A proactive, positive explanation of test data is much better than excuses after the fact. Principals need to establish a school climate where testing is comfortably accepted.

Use the diagnostic tests to identify barriers and explain what is needed and then advocate loudly for the personnel and resources to help all children be successful.

Tip 52

Reduce Paper Use

Don't let mail or paperwork cross your desk more than once. Those principals who are buried with paperwork haven't figured that out. Learn to determine what type of mail requires immediate action, what can be filed, and what should be tossed. Good secretaries pride themselves in their ability to sort the mail for the principal.

Work with your staff to determine ways of eliminating excess paperwork. Encourage teachers to reduce the number of dittoes and worksheets they use. Help them learn to teach using hands-on activities, varying their lessons to address the learning styles of all their students.

The electronic, online age requires less paper. Don't make backup paper copies for work that is saved online. Requisitions, purchase orders, and numerous other record-keeping and business functions should be completed electronically. Student cumulative records can be processed and maintained online, eliminating the need for bulky folders and more file cabinets. Learn to create forms and surveys for teachers and parents using e-mail and the Internet. Not only will less paper be used, the results can be tallied much more efficiently. The data collected electronically can be more easily disaggregated to give you information about your students' performance and parent feedback that can be used to drive decisions regarding instruction and curriculum.

Principals need to advocate the administration of state and national online tests using their state computer networks.

Think of the paper that would be saved. These tests could be administered by the states according to law and regulations on similar dates, with results returned to the schools much more expediently than current practice. Fall and spring administrations of tests would provide principals and teachers a baseline for analyzing student learning and growth during the academic year.

Principals who create unnecessary paperwork for their staff will be unpopular. Less is more.

TIP 53

Help Teachers Become Data Users

Principals must encourage and support teachers to use data to drive their instructional decisions. This can be done by

- Arranging common planning time for teams of teachers
- Monitoring lesson plans
- Demonstrating and modeling how to use data to guide instruction
- Teaching staff how to disaggregate data and examine trends
- Using the support of experts and consultants
- Engaging in ongoing professional development activities
- Empowering master teachers to work with others
- Sharing best practices demonstrating how data analysis can lead to higher levels of student and adult performance and achievement
- Networking with other schools, particularly those with similar demographics, to identify common obstacles and strategies for success

Teachers often go to principals with ideas, opinions, and complaints on a multitude of topics. But it's important to avoid being swayed in inappropriate directions, which you can do by stating, "Show me the data that support that position, problem, or opinion." When individuals in my school have only their opinions or their personal feelings as supportive data for a position, they know I won't listen to or support them.

I've also learned to question who and how many constitute "everyone" when a staff member or parent brings a complaint. If truly everyone on my staff (50+ adults) is upset about the resource schedule, I will be more willing to review the problem than if "everyone" represents only two or three people. When a parent informs me that "everyone" dislikes Miss Jones, I question who they mean by "everyone." Show me the data and you get my attention. With good data, I can make an informed decision.

Likewise, teachers need to become savvy data consumers. They need to become more reliant on data than on only their instincts and intuition. Doing so will enable them to better analyze and examine trends and student needs. Decisions will be better in the end.

Tip 54

Use Technology

We live in a high-tech world. Children in our schools will experience and live with accessible technologies that we've never dreamed about. Principals must set the tone and model expectations about learning and technology usage for the school.

At a time when some states and districts are issuing laptops or handheld computers to every student, it is old fashioned for a principal to write on a legal pad for a secretary to retype or format later. I use a laptop while writing classroom observation reports in classrooms. Colleagues and I share documents and beam messages and schedules in meetings via our palm pilots. Cell phones are a must. Time is not wasted.

Throw out the legal pads!

6

Parents and Community

Your children need your presence more than your presents.

—Reverend Jesse Jackson

Tip 55

Engage the Community

The Ohio Association of Elementary School Administrators annually sponsors a program titled "Supervision With a Principal," better known as SWAP. Participating principals invite a guest from the community to shadow them for a day. In return, the principal swaps and learns the work world of the invited guest. At a celebration luncheon, it is enlightening to listen to the perspectives of community people, many of whom haven't set foot in a school since they were students.

One of my guests, Ed Clum, operated a homeless shelter and food kitchen near my school. After our SWAP experience, he continued to show interest in the kids in my school. Over time, he helped establish an afterschool tutoring program using community volunteers—before afterschool programs gained popularity and became widespread.

Along with Rosemary Hajost, a retired teacher and business owner, we originated the West After School Center, Inc., a nonprofit 501(c)(3) incorporation, that now owns and operates a $350,000 facility directly across the street from our school's playground. Plans now call for the original tutoring program, which for five years was housed in a neighboring church, to expand by creating many other services for students and families of our school. An independent, community board of directors directs operations, policy, and procedures. Much of the financial support for construction and operation comes from community donations and volunteers.

The effects of this strong community support have helped transform the school. At times, I have had to devote skillful negotiation, guidance, and sensitivity to people's egos and maintain direct involvement to sustain the initiatives. But it has been worth it because kids have received numerous benefits from community mentors—positive role models who have developed positive personal relationships with kids that will reap rewards for years to come.

And that is the key! Our program has evolved over time to produce a beautiful, independently owned community center. But the focus has always been, and always will remain, on the at-risk children who need a friend, who seek attention. With the right connection to positive role models, they will become better students, high school graduates, and productive citizens. Supporting programs such as this is what a caring, engaged community should be about.

And an effective principal must have vision and take a lead in making things like this happen.

Tip 56

Be the Cheerleader for Your School

Go to any college sports event and watch the cheerleaders. What should you see? Bright, enthusiastic, talented, athletic men and women who are the epitomes of "be true to your school." They maintain their positive optimism through victory and defeat. They know how to motivate others to support the team.

Elementary and middle level principals could benefit from cheerleader training. Learning how to project a positive image, being gracious and cheerful in times of defeat (and victory), and knowing how to "sell" a school are all timeless lessons for principals.

Many principals don't like to "toot their own horns." If you don't, few others will. The public *must* hear the good things that happen each day in our schools. Gather your colleagues and, as a team, cheer together! Let your community hear about your school. Make this a priority.

Just like with the cheerleaders, if you are a loyal believer, good things *can and will* happen. You can overcome the odds. But you have to work at it. You can become a winner. Start cheering!

Tip 57

Be Accountable and Advocate for School Resources

I've never met a principal who was afraid to be held accountable, but most I know resent being held accountable when the playing field isn't level. Who'd ever expect to see Harvard play football in the same league as Ohio State?

Both Harvard and Ohio State support football teams. But they do so from widely different levels of support and expectations. Football is a big-ticket item at Ohio State. The athletic department and particularly the head coach are accountable for much more than their counterparts at Harvard. And alumni accept the difference. Until Harvard spends an equivalent amount and recruits equally talented coaches and players, no reasonable football fan would assume they would compete against each other or be compared in the same ways.

Use the same analogy for our schools. If the U.S. public expects all schools to be held to the same standard, it must provide adequate and equitable facilities and resources, competitive salaries, and comparatively trained staffs. Principals must be accountable to their communities and make citizens aware of the inadequacies and unfairness of a system that continually privileges the rich over the poor. Principals have the social power and influence to make a difference. Speak up and make people aware of the realities we know so well.

Tip 58

Maintain a Current Web Site for the School

When I was trying to explain directions from Columbus to our school for a young teacher candidate, she said, "Oh, I already know the directions. I found them on the Internet. I downloaded them while I was getting acquainted with your school while reviewing your Web site."

Ever spend some time surfing the net and browsing other schools' Web sites? You can find some wonderful ideas or you can find information that hasn't been updated in years. That's like driving past a school on Valentine's Day and seeing a notice on the school marquee wishing everyone a Happy New Year. Too bad no one in the school saw a need to keep things current.

Having a school Web site is a great way to advertise your school's accomplishments. And Web sites have become an important public relations tool. Post student work on the Web. Place pictures, once you have permission. Describe your school's vision and mission. The Web is the first choice for finding information for more and more people, and effective principals are using its many features to advance their schools. Newsletters that traditionally went home on plain paper come alive with movement and sound on the Web. Many Web sites contain interesting, informational videos. What a great way to communicate your verbal message to those of your school community who can't read. And don't assume illiterate people don't have access to the Web. Ever notice how some of the most unread adults you know seem to have cell phones, pagers, DVD players, and all the other latest electronic gadgets?

My staff thought they couldn't survive without hard copies of staff bulletins, memos, and other interschool communications. They almost revolted the day I informed them my communications would be sent via e-mail or available on the school Web site. That forced some of them to learn to use their computers more effectively. But we now save paper and have a more efficient and reliable means of communication. Change takes time, but I think very few would want to return to the use of the old fashioned, blue-ink ditto machine.

Principals need to learn how to post information to their Web site. The quality of the information on the school Web site is a reflection of the school's interest in helping parents and the larger community stay informed.

TIP 59

Develop a Repertoire of Parent Involvement Activities

The research is clear. Students do better in school when their parents are involved. But today, students live in home environments much different than baby boomers experienced. The biological, intact, two-parent family is now the minority. Ozzie and Harriett don't live in many neighborhoods anymore.

Finding ways to include and involve busy parents in their children's education is an ongoing challenge for principals. Best practices are always shared at workshops and conferences. The following list is just a sampling of ideas that can enhance parent involvement:

- Parent contracts (see the sample in Form 6.1)
- Parent luncheons; classroom visitations
- Parent breakfasts (donuts for dads, muffins for moms)
- Grandparent, grandfriend days
- Homework planners
- Friday folders
- Phone calls home with positive messages
- Walking kindergarteners home (scheduled home visits)
- Videos of Guide to Grade, Open House, Meet the Teacher Activities
- Videos and recordings of newsletters for parents who can't read or see
- Curriculum nights

- Parenting workshops
- New parent nights
- School tours
- Parent surveys
- Invitations to assemblies
- Career-sharing days, guest lecturers
- Clean-up days
- Realtor and childcare and babysitting information
- School spirit clothing
- Awards celebrations
- Read-ins
- Refrigerator magnets with calendars of events, phone numbers, and so on

Be creative and share your ideas with others. Parents are important customers. Adopt a customer-friendly attitude and do what it takes to make sure your customers come back and get involved.

Form 6.1   Parent Contract With West Elementary School

Lancaster City Schools

We (I), the undersigned, agree to the following educational challenge and understand that fulfilling our (my) contractual obligation will increase the possibility of our (my) child(ren)'s educational success. It is further understood and agreed upon that such efforts on our (my) part may result in more involvement in our (my) child(ren)'s education and create a better learning environment at home. We (I) hold all parties responsible for sound educational opportunities and look forward to the enjoyment of helping in the implementation of the aforementioned opportunities.

Parent Signature _____   **Date** _____

Parent Signature _____   **Date** _____

I agree to do my best in helping the above-signed parent (Mom and/or Dad) to do their part in fulfilling each challenge listed below.

Child Signature _____   **Child's Teacher** _____

Item 1   *Read to your child or have your child read to you at least 15 minutes per day.*
_____ Yes   _____ No

Item 2   *Attend at least two of nine PTO meetings (check as attended).*
Sept. 7 _____   Oct. 5 _____   Nov. 2 _____   Dec. 7 _____   Jan. 4 _____
Feb. 1 _____   March 1 _____   Apr. 5 _____   May 3 _____

Item 3   *Call the school between 8–9 a.m. if your child is absent due to illness.*

Item 4   *Communicate with your child's teacher using the homework planner and monitor your child's assignments. (Grades 2–6 only).*

Item 5   *Confer with your child's teacher in person (or by phone if absolutely impossible to be at school) during first-quarter parent-teacher conference.*
November 2 or 3, 2002 (Kindergarten) _____ Yes
November 9, 2002 (K–6) _____ Yes

Item 6   *Make sure your child arrives on time to school between 8:35–8:55 and is picked up between 3:30–3:40.*

Item 7   *Read school and teacher newsletters and share information with your child.*
_____ Yes   _____ No

Optional: Volunteer at a PTO event or offer to volunteer in the class at least once this year. Ask your child's teacher how you can help. Please return the signed contract by October 5, 2002.

A CELEBRATION SPAGHETTI DINNER WILL BE HELD IN EARLY MAY 2003 FOR THOSE FAMILIES WHO HAVE COMPLETED THE PARENT CONTRACT.

Source: Used with the permission of West Elementary School.

Tip 60

Learn How to Work With the Media

Many who have experienced a crisis at their schools say that working with the media as the emergency vehicles pull away can be even more stressful than the actual crisis. Principals must understand that they will frequently have to speak to the media. They must practice and know what they want to say.

There are many workshops and training programs for working with the media. I've always found listening and talking with colleagues at principals' conferences to be very worthwhile. Listen to their stories. Learn from their authentic experiences. Do whatever works best. Get yourself prepared for working with the media as you conduct planning for an emergency. Both go hand in hand.

Designate a spokesperson in the event of an emergency. Designate backups. Develop your plan with support from the district communications office. Get to know the people in your local media before there is a problem. Build relationships. Pay forward.

There are times when reporters will call to ask a principal for an opinion about various educational issues. State and national principal associations annually publish platforms and position papers for their members, developed by principals for principals. Have these free publications close by in a file for easy reference. If the reporter challenges the position, you'll have the best thinking and support of your colleagues as a resource.

Train your secretary to field calls. Let the reporter know you'll call him or her back if you feel unprepared. Buy time. Study up on the issue. Call a colleague or your association office for advice. Prepare a few talking points, return the call, and don't stray from your issues and the remarks you want quoted.

Learn to dress for the lights and staging of television. Particular colors and styles of clothing help create a professional look. Learn how to style your hair and wear your glasses. Request time to practice before speaking into microphones and cameras. Make sure to have a copy of the comments and points you want to make.

Don't let the media intimidate you. Relax. Principals are the experts. Learn to converse with the media representative as you would a friend.

Tip 61

Collect and Tell Stories

Principals are frequently asked to speak. It's one of the important things principals do, either formally or informally. So start collecting a repertoire of good stories now and master the art of storytelling.

Ever watch the masters on television talk shows? They catch their listeners' attention by engaging them in stories—personal, factual, true, or make believe. They also tell good jokes or include humor while they talk. It's what show business is all about, and there are lessons to be learned by educators, especially principals, by observing those in the entertainment industry.

Professional storytellers master the art of weaving powerful messages in their tales. They can keep young children spellbound as their fantasy unfolds. Paul Harvey is a master with twists and turns in his radio show, "The Rest of the Story." I've pulled my car to the side of the road numerous times to listen.

People listen to great stories. Amazing power lies in the story of our schools . . . and in you!

Tip 62

Talk to Lawmakers

Just as it's important to learn to work with the media, it's vital to talk with state and national legislators. Most principals don't do this enough.

Most elected representatives in state capitals and Washington, DC, acknowledge education issues to be one of their top priorities. But unless they were board members, teachers, or administrators, few have regular contact with schools. Some haven't been in an elementary or middle level school since they were students. Invite your representative to visit. Let him or her understand your concerns and issues from your point of view in your environment. Point out the wonderful things that happen daily. Build relationships.

State and national principal associations conduct regular training to help members address issues with lawmakers. They help principals understand the many pressures of elected representatives and how they are constantly being lobbied by constituents. Associations identify legislative positions and work to both affect and effect laws. They provide information and access to resources that are valued by both principals and the elected officials. Become involved and sign up to participate in state and national legislative electronic networks.

Learn to work through legislative aides when direct access with the elected representative is not possible. Many times, when aides privately have the ears of their bosses, they can influence and make your points even better than if you personally spoke to the representative.

Don't be intimidated by the pomp and grandeur of state and national capitals. Principals are the experts. Remember that representatives work for their communities and need to hear from you. Advocate for what you need in your schools to do your job effectively. Avoid being a whiner and complainer. Address the issues. Make this a priority. Focus on what is best for children and learning.

Tip 63

Be Active in Your Community

I've always thought it was important to live in the community where I worked. I never wanted to ask voters to approve taxes that I wouldn't be assessed myself. Some principalships have residential requirements, but those appear to be fewer and fewer. What works for me in my location might not work elsewhere. You need to be able to establish a comfortable home. Extremely high housing costs might prevent principals from living in some school districts, others might not be safe, and remote rural areas often lack adequate housing and services. Regardless, I strongly encourage principals to become active and accept leadership positions within their school communities.

Join service clubs. Attend weekend ballgames and events at the high school. Interact with people. Get to know them and know things about them. Shop in the local stores. Vote. Assume leadership roles when possible.

Principals have far more influence and social power where they live and work than they realize. Many of the little things they do enable them to build relationships with more people than anyone else in the school district. Effective principals work diligently to make themselves known and to pay their dues. Over time, they reap the benefits—for their children, their schools, and their future.

Tip 64

Call 911 When Necessary

Once you've been assigned principal of a school, invite the chief of police, fire chief, fire marshal, and key emergency medical team members to visit with you at school. Ask them to review your operational procedures and emergency evacuation plans. Establish a close working relationship with them and people of their service departments. Schedule frequent visits. They need to become familiar with you, your physical plant, and your needs.

The fable about the boy who cried wolf has stayed with me since I first learned it. As a result, I know I've hesitated making requests for assistance, not wanting to abuse my calls or have others think I couldn't handle emergencies. Making the right call is often difficult, especially when you can't reach the parent of a young child. When in doubt, I've learned to call the authorities for help.

In and across states, principals are mandated by law to report suspected child abuse. Many times the decision the principal will face is not clearly black or white. Making a call for assistance sometimes has political fallout and creates strained relationships with difficult parents. It is better to seek help and err than to waste invaluable time and be criticized for inaction later. Having a good, familiar relationship with my nearby emergency service agencies helps reassure my uncertainty.

Besides the local emergency personnel, every effective principal needs a mentor, critical friend, or colleague he or she can call anytime, anywhere, for any reason. Place these people on speed dial. Make sure your secretarial staff knows that they always get through to you. The old adage, "two heads are better than one," is quite true. Seek help. Principals can't do it all in isolation. Don't be shy about asking for help,

Tip 65

Listen

This one is difficult for some principals, especially me! But you simply have no choice but to become a good listener if you want to be an effective principal.

Behind their backs, people describe principals who talk only about themselves or appear not to listen as being egotistical and arrogant. In any good conversation, give-and-take sharing transpires between the parties. If one dominates, the other shuts down. Principals must know how to listen and skillfully ask questions that draw others into the conversation. They need to know how to listen with their ears and watch with their eyes. They learn to hear between the lines what people really mean to say. People enjoy working with principals who relate to what they are feeling as well as what they are saying.

Principals who are the best conversationalists are great commiserators. Focusing on how people feel helps the principal draw them out and open a conversation. It helps develop trust and connectedness. Empathetic principals know how to listen and ask questions that show they care, convey recognition and value, and show respect for the individual.

More than simply listening, a principal must draw out *all* voices. You must elicit different viewpoints. Schedule informal interviews with varied members of your constituency (i.e., former parents, former students, neighbors of the school) to gain insight and information.

When someone enters my office with a question, I force myself to stop what I'm doing (typing, reading, focusing on paperwork, etc.). I always look them in the eye, smile, and focus on what they say as well as how they look saying it. I listen and read their body language. I summarize or paraphrase what I hear. It's always hard to be interrupted. But principals will be formally and informally evaluated negatively if they can't listen.

Tip 66

Celebrate Successes

We don't celebrate enough of the good things in schools. And when we do, we don't always think to invite the right people to the party! So you're thinking, "Who should be invited?" "What should be celebrated?"

This question should be answered partially by staff and parents and adapted to district norms and policies. Students themselves, through the student council, should be asked to help define successes at their school and how they should be celebrated.

Here are some typical celebratory occasions:

- End-of-the-year awards assemblies
- Athletic team victories
- Extra- and co-curricular activities competitions
- Retirements
- Group test achievement
- Specific events and recognitions

Too often, celebratory events take place within the school with limited participation—even from parents. Celebrating with just staff and students, although not a negative thing, does not spread the good word and may not provide sufficient recognition for teacher and student effort. Principals need to prepare a list of dignitaries, guests, and people who should be invited to share special celebrations with the school population. Inform your secretary how to select from the list to send invitations. This list might include the following:

- Elected representatives (local, state, national)
- The mayor
- School board members
- Central office administration
- Other principals
- Professional association and union representatives
- Members of the local clergy
- Media personnel
- Business partners
- Support personnel from related services and emergency personnel
- Volunteers
- Parents
- Special friends of the school

Effective principals also create many ways to privately celebrate the success of individuals. These might include the following items:

- Personal phone calls
- Handwritten notes
- Computer-generated congratulatory cards
- Attendance at private parties
- Personal compliments
- Personal handwritten comments on grade cards
- Certificates

At state and national professional conferences, principals continuously share best practices with many more and better ideas for celebrations than outlined in this book. Make sure to attend.

The tip is that effective principals focus on celebrating the good things that happen in their schools. They work with others to plan appropriate celebratory events. They plan in advance how to invite others to share. They acknowledge success and effort. They share the good word.

TIP 67

Encourage an International Perspective

For their future success, American children need to attain a worldview. They need to learn to eliminate stereotypes and appreciate the richness and dignity of world cultures. Many schools start close to home by developing relationships with other schools to bridge the diversities of urban, suburban, and rural schools. In the context of the larger world, students need guidance from an early age to help them balance their expression of patriotism against a growing world perception of U.S. arrogance. They need to understand world history, geography, political climates, religions, health issues, markets, free and fair trade, and economic investment and growth. They need opportunities to learn other languages. Young students need to learn how and why others in the world view the United States the way they do. They need to understand propaganda. They must become critical thinkers and consumers and appreciate what it takes to protect the American way of life.

These issues must be addressed so they have important meaning and relevance in students' lives. Principals, teachers, and students need to help build real, authentic interpersonal connections with educational leaders and students in schools in other countries. They need to write, talk, trade, and share cultural values and ideas with people throughout the world. Principals can enable their staffs and students to use the Internet and other media to establish ongoing communication networks. Everyone will be enriched.

This work with students will model what is desperately needed for adults in many U.S. communities. Some principals will argue they don't have time, considering their many other mandates and societal demands. But effective principals have already been working at establishing communication networks and educational exchanges. They understand the value of improving international relationships. They are preparing their students now for success in an adult world.

7

Taking Care of the Organization

A child is a person who is going to carry on what you have started. He is going to move in and take over your church, schools, universities, and corporations. The fate of humanity is in his hands.

—Abraham Lincoln

Tip 68

Don't Overlook the Little Details

Always be the first to get your paperwork returned to your boss. If there are fifteen schools in the district, it's likely that the boss or a designee keeps track of the order of the returned responses from principals. Don't let your procrastination or inattention to the little details put you on the list of those who are always last, or worse, always late. Keep track of meeting dates, upcoming events, expectations, and responsibilities in efficient ways. Keep a to-do list and update it daily. When another principal calls and makes a request, attend to it right away. When asked for a reference letter, surprise the requester with your fast response. Write thank you notes within two days. Acknowledge those around you and be courteous and friendly with all people who interact with the school. Be reliable, efficient, and trustworthy with your attention to the little details. If you don't stay on top of them, they accumulate and become big issues with others.

With teachers, I grow frustrated with those who fail to turn in lesson plans for review, lack consideration for others' schedules, report late to assigned duties, consistently fail to respond to paperwork requests, put off calling parents with discipline concerns, and so on—the little details that, when not completed, become big items of frustration for others—especially for me or my secretary.

Principals who fail to focus on the little details of scheduling events, fail to inform people exactly what they expect, get to meetings late, forget to ask about a sick relative, and so forth, gain unfavorable reputations and don't get the most from their staffs. The little things make a big difference. Focus on them, and make sure they get done.

Beginning principals need to work with a mentor to help understand, visualize, and plan the little details that make a big difference. Planning and intuitive thinking are vital. Who will be there to open the doors for the PTA carnival? Who makes sure the building is secure and everyone has gone home? Who makes coffee and gets donuts for an inservice meeting? Who sets up a staff meeting and arranges a room? Failure to anticipate and think through the little details can overwhelm, destroy, and bury a principal. Having a critical friend observe and evaluate what you're doing is safer than waiting for the boss to do it.

Write daily or weekly electronically distributed staff bulletins (take a look at the sample bulletin that follows). Include details everyone on the staff must know for the school to operate smoothly. Let the staff contribute ideas and identify the information that is most helpful. Teach people what you want them to know by concentrating on what you write, and explain things the little things that make a difference.

Sample Staff Bulletin

WEST ELEMENTARY SCHOOL
STAFF BULLETIN

Dr. Paul G. Young, Principal
March 1, 2002

March	FRI	1	Elementary Principals' Mtg., 9:30 a.m., ESC Practice Spelling Bee, 1:15 p.m. at Cedar Hts., *Dr. Y. and grade level winners and alternates*
	MON	4	Proficiency Testing begins (MWF)
	TUE	5	WASC Special Committee Luncheon, noon, Country Club, Dr. Y.
	WED	6	Student Council Meeting, 8:35, Room 23 West After School Center Board of Directors Mtg., 9:30, Room 1
	THU	7	IAT Mtg., 7:45 Gr. 5-B; 8:15 Gr. 5-B Principals' Mtg. 9:30 ESC; 6th Grade Outdoor Ed. Mtg., 6:30 p.m. PTO Mtg., 7:00 P.M.
	FRI	8	Staff Meeting, 8:15 a.m., *Supt. visiting*
	SAT	9	Lancaster Eagle Gazette Regional Spelling Bee, 10:00 a.m., OU-L
	MON	11	Discipline Committee Meeting, 8:15 a.m., library Proficiency testing continues (MWF)
	TUE	12	Venture Capital Comm. Mtg., 8:15 a.m. RSVP Parent Meeting, 7:30 p.m.
	WED	13	Johnny Magic Safety Show, 2:30 p.m. K-6, 30 minutes, m-p room
	THU	14	IAT Mtg., 7:45 2-A; 8:15 Gr. TBA World's Largest Concert, 1-1:30 p.m., Music...Pass It On!
	MON-FRI	18-22	RSVP Program
	THU	21	IAT Mtg., 7:45 Gr. 5-B; 8:15 Gr. 5-B Music Program, Grades 1, 2 & 3, at Sherman, 7 p.m.
	FRI	22	Staff Meeting, 8:15 a.m. library
	MON	25	ASDO Team Mtg., 8:15 a.m.
	THU	28	IAT Mtg., 7:45 Gr. 1-A; 8:15 Gr. 1-B Kids on the Block, 9 a.m.—1 p.m., library End of the 3rd Nine Weeks (46 days due)
	FRI	29	Good Friday, No School
April	MON-FRI	1-5	SPRING BREAK. No classes NAESP Board of Directors Meeting & National Convention, San Antonio, TX
	MON-WED	8-10	NAESP National Convention, San Antonio, TX. *Dr. Young attending*
	TUE	9	Special Ed. Staff Mtg., 3:45 p.m., ESC
	THU	11	IAT Mtg., 7:45 Gr. 3-A; 8:15 Gr. 3-A PTO Mtg., 7:00 p.m. (slate of officers presented)

Information Item

- The Family Night Kickoff for the Running Start Program will be Tuesday, April 16, 2002, 7:00 p.m.
- Dr. XXXXXXXX fell and broke her leg last week while preparing to leave home for a visit to one of our schools. At this point, further information is vague. You may want to send her a get well wish at kkkkkkkkk@aol.com
- Proficiency Test Snacks: If you haven't done so already, make a call this morning and arrange assistance from your room parent/s for snacks for the class during the proficiency test. Also, make sure that students have breakfast, either at home, or here at school the next two weeks.
- On March 15, students grades 3-6 are invited to Lancaster High School for a preview of *Annie*, the high school musical which takes place the following weekend.
- There will not be any tutoring classes held for our students the weeks of March 4 and 11 due to the proficiency tests.
- XXXX YYYYYY, a representative for Horace Mann, will be available for those interested on Monday, April 15 during the lunch periods.
- Please remind students NOT to open doors to our school to anyone, even other parents. When using restrooms out of our sight, sometimes they forget. This reminder is for everyone's safety.
- REMINDER—If a student uses the restroom under your watch, make sure they have a pass (laminated pass, etc. with your name on it) signifying they have your permission to be in the hallways.
- REMINDER: Our Literacy Specialists are available to assist with your needs on testing days. VVVV BBBB is only here a.m. The literacy schedule will not run on testing days. See them to arrange their help!

**The 11th Annual
Early Childhood Conference**
Friday, March 22, 7:30-4:00 p.m.
Ohio University-Lancaster

Sponsored by the Fairfield County Early Childhood Council

LUCKY TICKET EVENT
Everyone Invited!
Lucky Ticket Drawings
50/50 Raffle
Basket Raffles
Sandwiches and Snacks
Saturday March 2, 2002; LHS Cafeteria
1:00 p.m. Shopping Time 2:00 p.m. Ticket Drawing
Stan Robinson is Master of Ceremonies

**Music Program
Grades 1, 2, & 3**
Disney Spectacular
Thursday, March 21, 2002
Performance at General
Sherman, 7:00 p.m. (line-up at 6:50)
Dress Rehearsal,
2:00 p.m., m-p room

See Mrs. VVVVVV if you can't attend so she can assign another adult to monitor your students and assist.

**World's Largest Concert
MUSIC...Pass It on!**
Thursday, March 14, 2002, WOSU

Millions of children from around the world will be participating. This year's program represents past and future Olympics host countries (Nagano Japan 98; Sydney, Australian. 00; Salt Lake City 02; Athens, Greece 04; Turin, Italy, 06; and Beijing, China 08) featuring different languages, world peace and unity.
Visit: www.MENC.org/guides/wk/2002/Front.html

37th Annual Children's Theatre Production
**Lancaster Arts and
Civic Club**
Presents
"The Frog Prince"

Dates:	Friday, March 22, 7:30 p.m. Saturday, March 23, 7:30 p.m. Sunday, March 24, 2:00 p.m.
Place:	Ohio University-Lancaster Jeffrey Wagner Theatre
Tickets	$3.00

*Tickets available March 4 at local Kroger stores
Proceed to benefit local charities*

VVVV BBBBBBB is the princess!

Source: Used with the permission of West Elementary School.

TIP 69

Organize the Office

Make a good first impression. All visitors form their first impressions of the school when they visit or call the office. Give consideration to the following recommendations:

- Designate a greeter. All visitors should be greeted with a smile, have their questions addressed, offered coffee or tea if waiting for an appointment, and made to feel important and valued.
- The person who answers the phone must be knowledgeable; have a pleasant, calm voice; and a professional command of the English language. All calls should be answered after no more than three rings.
- Provide comfortable seating and reading material for waiting guests.
- Instruct school personnel to conduct conversations elsewhere. Visitors do not need to be subjected to gossip or confidential information. Remove children awaiting discipline conferences to another area.
- Remove clutter and open window shades to allow sunshine to brighten the environment.
- Make sure the office is clean—remove dust from corners and under computers, clean windows, wax floors, touch up paint scrapes.
- Organize the necessary papers on bulletin boards in an attractive manner. Place notices of interest to the public in clear view. Keep information current.

- Decorate the office with attractive seasonal items. Student work and art is always appropriate and of interest to visitors. Display the good things that happen in the school.
- All additional rooms in the office complex need to be neat and orderly for public view.
- Organize the filing system, secure confidential records, and provide access to mail and materials for all personnel.
- Arrange the layout of desks and equipment so that personnel can monitor all people coming and going from the office. The arrangement should be user friendly and facilitate the busy work that takes place.
- Use volunteers. Make sure they have training and continuous monitoring of their work, especially if they have access to sensitive information.
- Schedule regular times to confer with the support personnel and the office staff. Plan and make sure everyone is on the same page with coming events and work assignments.
- Clarify your expectations. People can't be expected to do good work if they haven't been told what to do.
- Reward the work of a super secretary!

Tip 70

Read and Respond to E-Mail

Like it or not, educators today communicate through electronic mail more than by using paper memos and conventional mail. Some complain that reading and writing e-mails makes them a slave to the computer. But many principals are technologically sophisticated, using their palm pilots, cellular phones, and other devices that enable them to be connected anywhere, anytime. They share files and beam messages during meetings while others wonder what is going on. Moreover, they have the potential of being more productive than their peers who continue using paper and pencil. And they save money each time they avoid buying a postal stamp.

Despite the conveniences of technology, e-mail seems to have increased the amount of communication for principals rather than making the workload less. Regardless, it is highly unlikely the world will retreat back to the "good old days." The same colleagues who complain that they haven't got time to read e-mail often refuse to invest in their own learning about technology, especially how best to use a computer. Some are still unable to compose a letter, type it, or address it without the aid of their secretaries. Some continue to use yellow legal pads, write memos in longhand, and require a secretary to type them up. This is double work. Everyone needs to learn to work smarter rather than harder. Principals who expect technology to be integrated throughout the school curriculum must fully use its potential in their work. They must model expectations for others.

Principals need to discipline themselves to read e-mail regularly throughout the workday, respond within a reasonable amount of time, and delete junk mail, all the while juggling many other responsibilities related to working with teachers, students, and parents. Nothing is more irritating than sending messages, expecting responses, and having a colleague fail to respond time after time. Often, those neglectful colleagues were the same individuals who never kept up with their traditional mail and paperwork. Be courteous, keep up, and respond to messages each day. Model an expectation for your staff as well.

Consider the tremendous amount of trees that can be saved! And what new communication devices will principals be using in the near future?

Tip 71

Return All Phone Messages the Same Day

When my superintendent informed principals that he expected all phone messages to be returned before we left for the day, I was frustrated. He said he understood how busy we all were, but why was he being so demanding? That evening, I thought about his expectation while jogging. After a good workout and giving his request a second consideration, it made sense. And it has become a daily goal to clear away all the pink "While You Were Out" notices and go home for the evening with a clean slate.

If my customers needed to speak with me, ask a question, register a complaint, seek information, or whatever, it must have been important to them or they would not have called. It is insensitive to be inconsiderate of their requests. Business people clearly understand that their customers will go somewhere else if they fail to respond. With school choice and alternative educational options becoming more widespread, principals must realize that their customers may go elsewhere, too. If we called a parent and left a message to call the school and they failed to do so, we would begin having all sorts of negative thoughts about the parent's attitude, responsibility, and interest in school. Why should they assume anything less about us?

This tip is a no-brainer! Return your calls on the same day. And make sure your secretary records all messages accurately, or get a voice mail system.

Tip 72

Write Notes Daily

As a beginning principal, I heard a veteran administrator advise everyone to write at least three notes each day. I've made it a goal since, and the returns on the investment of my time and energy have been more than worth it. Purchase nice stationery, or have some personalized note cards made, and focus on identifying special things that people do to help make the school improve and run smoothly. Write notes to teachers, support staff, volunteers, parents, children, community members, your boss—anyone who positively impacts your school and your job. Reinforce your expectations and the wonderful things you observe in a quiet, personal manner. Clip articles from the newspaper and include copies with your note. People will love the recognition and attention from you.

The fact that you take the time to write a note in your own handwriting makes it very personal. My southpaw handwriting is atrocious, and writing becomes very tedious for me. My secretary often has to translate my messages for others. But receivers appreciate the effort, thought, and recognition. I see my notes in staff planbooks, in students' homes on refrigerators, and in scrapbooks. They become treasured items. My file is full of notes I value from others.

Write three notes each day!

Tip 73

Keep a Special Idea File

My staff loves it when I return from a professional conference or meeting. They've come to laugh and expect some new ideas and projects. I've had to learn to tone down my impetuous enthusiasm and introduce innovations and practices over time, during teachable moments. So they won't be forgotten or lost, I collect and file ideas for future reference. They'll be there in the special idea file for easy access at opportune moments. Keep notes, artifacts, and information in whatever form works best for you.

I also collect books, recordings, and advertisements. You never know when a moment will present itself when people are eager for innovative ideas.

I've often been in administrative meetings when colleagues would discuss a particular new topic and wonder where they might seek more information. I always keep a copy of every state and national professional conference program. When I review the session offerings, I can usually find a colleague who has experience with the topic. A simple telephone call or e-mail connects you with tremendous amounts of information, experience, advice, and best practices.

Get organized when you first become a principal. Collect ideas. You never know when you will need them.

Tip 74

Maintain Eye Contact

Eye contact is important. I've known too many principals who didn't seem to understand how important this could be to their success. I always notice the focus, intensity, and interest shown in others' eyes when I am speaking. It reflects whether they are interested and listening to me. The eyes tell so much about a person.

I have reservations about prospective teaching candidates who can't look me in the eye during interviews. And when students won't make eye contact, I look for reasons why. Are they embarrassed, untruthful, not listening, hiding something, or afraid of any number of things? The same with their parents. What does it convey when the principal cannot make eye contact with others?

It is equally important, before rushing to judgment, to know the cultural contexts of members of your learning community, particularly students and parents. Children may come from cultures that consider making eye contact to be disrespectful or insulting. A lowered gaze may be meant as a mark of humility or respect.

Principals are busy people. There are those who need to speak with us, some of whom can't get to the point of a story. As expert multitaskers, principals are capable of doing several things at once, but we must remember to focus eyes and attention when others speak to us. This little act conveys much and helps validate the speakers and their concerns.

The ability to maintain eye contact can be a valuable strength in tense situations. I've observed principals who could correct students' inappropriate behavior, challenge angry adults, or calm injured students using nothing more than the look in their eyes.

Find a critical friend. Ask for a critique of your eye contact with others. Don't dismiss this important aspect of your interpersonal communications.

Tip 75

Don't Write Memos While Angry

I've learned this tip through numerous personal experiences. Never send a memo or an e-mail that was written when you were angry or frustrated. It will come back to haunt you. I've had too many conferences with employees and their union representatives where memos I had written were challenged. The issue I was attempting to clarify or the point I was trying to make got lost when the tables turned and my anger or frustration became the focus. It is always better to have a colleague critique what you wrote. Remember, e-mails and memos become public documents, so don't write anything that you wouldn't want the world to read. Don't burn your bridges. The person you write a nasty memo to today may be your boss tomorrow. Phrase your comments in a professional manner. Buy time. Take a deep breath. Go run five miles. Put the nasty memo aside, cool off, read it when you've calmed down, and revise it.

I know colleagues who wrote what they thought were humorous but sarcastic comments in staff communications, later to see them become the subject of contract challenges and disciplinary actions. Not all people share the same senses of humor, and once something has been written and sent, it has strange ways of showing up when you least want it.

Others I know write nasty messages via e-mail. Court cases affirm that these are public property. Others can exercise legal rights to retrieve what you've written. Be careful. Think twice before you touch the "send" key.

I keep copies of nasty notes written by frustrated colleagues as reminders of what not to do. I imagine many others do the same. Don't write them. Focus on positive thoughts.

Tip 76

Know the Law

This is such common sense. Yet too many principals appear to believe they can make a mistake and ask for forgiveness later. I don't want to be asking forgiveness in a courtroom.

Laws change. Stay current. Your state professional association staff is a valuable resource. They provide updates, seminars, and workshops that should keep every principal in the know.

Principals must know the interpretation, requirements, and ramifications of many policies, mandates, and laws—student registration, custody, administration of medication, records release, reporting of suspected abuse, special education, and directory information to name a few. Stay informed. Read. Attend seminars. Seek input from authorities. You cannot be negligent. Know your responsibilities and rights. Make sure those reporting to you know the same. Always act in the best interest of other people. Make sure you have the highest levels of legal protection.

Relax. Your chances of being sued are less if you stay well informed of the law.

Tip 77

Ride Your School Buses

Am I ever thankful my mentor suggested this in my first principalship. In addition to observing where the kids lived, the skill of the driver, and the students' behavior, I learned the names of many of the country roads and highways as well as the geographic layout of the district.

My bus rides prepared me far beyond my expectations on a Friday afternoon when Bus 6 was struck by a garbage truck that had lost its brakes, descending out of control down a hill miles from the school on a rural road.

I was about ready to go home and change for the Friday evening football game when calls began coming from parents asking if the bus would be late. Soon after, a call came from the central office about the accident. Immediately, I started calling other parents, learning which students were already home, trying to determine who remained on the bus. I was able to visualize the terrain of the accident site and remember the students who would be remaining on the bus. I was relieved to learn that the dozen children still on board were safe and uninjured and quickly began reassuring their anxious parents when I called them. I can imagine the inadequacy and the incredible confusion I would have felt not knowing the lay of the land. I have the utmost respect for the driver, the most seriously injured person of the tragedy, whose quick thinking saved the life of the student exiting the bus as well as the children still on board.

The lessons of that experience have remained with me ever since. Drivers appreciate my interest in riding with them and the support I provide. I learn so much. I have the opportunity to listen to the driver's interests and concerns, and together we identify potential problems related to routing and student behavior before they become major issues.

Principals desperately want to focus on instructional leadership. Great, but don't underestimate issues related to bus safety and employee relations. A serious tragedy will haunt you forever. I came as close to losing kids as I ever want.

Tip 78

Recognize Spouses and Family Members

Take advantage of every opportunity to recognize the spouses and family members of your staff. Get them on your side. You need them to be supportive of the comprehensive work of the school. Teachers work long hours, grade papers, write lesson plans, support evening and weekend school activities, and engage in their own learning—most often on their own time at the expense of their families and personal time. If the spouse complains, it will make it difficult for the colleague to commit to the job.

Whenever you have the time in public forums, verbally thank your staff's spouses and families. Send them notes of appreciation. Include them in social gatherings. Inquire about kids and relatives and show interest in the spouse's work.

When the family at home is happy and supportive, chances are the colleague will be at school. Always do what you can to help that happen.

Tip 79

Always Make the Superintendent Look Good

School district politics can be nasty! People love to blame the administrators for much of what they do not like, and in smaller districts, rightfully or wrongfully, that usually means the superintendent or a central office designee's decisions are the constant subject of discussion. Too often, principals fall prey to the garbage network and get sucked into saying things and offering opinions that they would be better off keeping to themselves.

Never say anything bad about your boss. Principals who aspire to become a central office administrator do themselves no benefit by cutting down their superiors. Instead, by making him or her look good, the boss becomes promotable, opening the position in the district you may have your eyes on. When you promote other people's good points, others will want you to stay around. It's simply a matter of choice.

I certainly don't advocate making an incompetent person look good. Be patient; they'll reveal their true colors over time, and you will not be a part of the mudslinging that is common in far too many districts.

Help your boss look good in various forums. Give him or her tips of things to say and heads-ups to problems you see on the horizon. I've always asked my teachers that if a problem occurs under their watch during the day, and they suspect I might receive a call from a parent, to give me their information first before they go home. I don't like surprise visits or phone calls from parents about things of which I have no knowledge or awareness. I don't think a superintendent does, either.

One way to always make the boss look good and remain in a position to support you is to keep him or her informed. When you suspect a serious problem with a parent or staff member, simply call or e-mail and give your information and side of the story first. Most will be able to hear it, and the situation can be diffused before it escalates further. But if time after time, the boss receives calls and problems about you or your school without any forewarning, eventually it will reflect poorly on you. You probably develop doubts about the capabilities of teachers who surprise you, so why wouldn't your superintendent have the same response about you?

Keep the boss informed. Bosses don't like surprises.

Tip 80

Become an Authority on Head Lice, Rashes, Infectious Diseases, and Medications

As a child I should probably have taken Ritalin or some other medication for my impulsive activity. I squirm and fidget and have difficulty focusing. According to the indicators for ADD or ADHD behaviors, I would qualify. Many times, while distributing medication, I've contemplated issuing one pill to the child and taking one for myself. I never dreamed I'd be responsible for a cabinet full of medications. And at times, my office resembles an emergency room.

Some colleagues have on-site clinics in their schools staffed by trained medical staffs. Wonderful arrangements have been developed so that families can receive free or reduced-rate medical assistance right in the schools. But far too many schools go without that support for students and parents. And responsibility for distribution of medication falls to the principal (or designee, most often the secretary).

Ever looked for head lice? Some people confuse dandruff, hair spray, and other things in hair to be lice. You had better make sure you know what you are observing before you call home and inform parents of their child's head lice. The ramifications of an inaccurate diagnosis are dreadful! I've been called everything—even when I was right! The same is true with many other common ailments. Yet it is better to err on behalf of the safety and welfare of others than to allow an infectious child to remain in school. Dealing with these issues can be a principal's worst problem. Trying to find a responsible adult to pick up a vomiting child is a close runner-up. Become knowledgeable and informed, even if you have other staff to assist. The buck often stops in your office.

One winter morning, when I was preparing a trombone solo for a local music club recital, a parent entered the school office with her tardy son. I quickly signed him in and sent him on to class. My secretary was in another room at the copier. "Ms. Jones" and I were alone. When she asked me if I was still practicing, without looking up from the attendance register, I quickly answered, "I certainly am!" Then it dawned on me that Ms. Jones had no idea I played trombone. I realized that what she was really asking, because she addressed me as "Dr. Young," was if I had another career as a physician. I don't think I ever did straighten her out as to why I could give her child Ritalin at school.

Learn everything you can about your students' medical needs.

Tip 81

Maintain the Highest Level of Character

Numerous times I've had students and parents approach me in the supermarket on weekends and comment about my wearing jeans. It is apparently hard for them to imagine me with clothes other than what they see me wearing at school. They are really surprised when they see me dressed for jogging. It is such a change from the way they typically see me. My clothes may change, but I want them always to "see" the character they know at school. That translates into some dos and don'ts for principal character building.

Do

- Become visible in the school community
- Support students in extracurricular activities
- Treat people as important customers, just as you want them to treat you
- Be consistent, display a calm demeanor, and be positive in all your interactions with others
- Be punctual and follow through with your commitments with others
- Display a strong sense of organization and attention to detail

Don't

- Frequent nightclubs or party with colleagues or community members
- Make derogatory comments about colleagues or community members
- Take other people for granted
- Cheat or be dishonest or unreliable in your work
- Underestimate the importance of displaying good character at all times

Principals begin their tenure with an assumption from others that they have the highest character and ethics. How they perform in front of others, day in and day out, either affirms and adds to that perception or erodes it. Value and protect your character with the utmost concern.

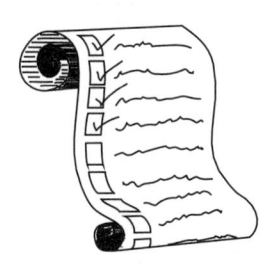

Tip 82

Tell the Truth

Principals, like everyone else, will find themselves in uncomfortable situations and be tempted to bend the truth or not tell all the facts. We wouldn't allow kids to be untruthful, to lie, and we can't either. But trust me: You'll be faced with many temptations.

When the boss calls to question something you might have said to an irate parent, tell the truth. Don't hold back factual information. Don't be afraid to make a mistake. Everyone does. Just don't let the big mistake be that of telling a lie.

I've twisted stories to make myself look good. I've hated myself afterwards. I don't lie well. I don't like it when people lie to me, especially when the culprit is a colleague.

It is also important to tell the truth about your school. If you need more resources or more staff or need to improve instruction, say so. It does little good to look the other way, be evasive, or cover up things that are wrong at your school. Be direct and honest when evaluating ineffective performance.

The truth is often hard to tell and to hear, but it builds deeper relationships and far greater trust in the organization.

TIP 83

Smile

I know too many people who get all fancied up to go out on the town and forget to put on one important item—a smile. How sad that they can't radiate in their beautiful attire.

In his bestseller, *The Tipping Point,* author Malcolm Gladwell cites an example of how infectious yawning can be. Try it! Next time you are with a group of people, yawn. Then observe those around you. It won't take long for others to do the same. It never fails. You can turn it into a game, and no one will know what you are doing. It may be a little more obvious, but try the same with a smile. Most often, with a smile comes eye contact, and your eyes may give your game away. But if you work with a group of frowners, try this little game and see if you can make a difference.

As stated numerous times in this book, principals set the tone for what happens in their schools. People look to the principal for how to handle situations. If the principal is visibly irritated and stressed, it is likely that others in the school will demonstrate the same demeanor. However, if the principal portrays a bright, can-do attitude, teachers, students, and parents will all thrive and feel confident. If they smile, others will reflect one back. This is such a simple tip but one often overlooked. Look in the mirror. What do you see? Besides your wrinkles, do the lines around the corners of your mouth curve up or down? Everyone at your school benefits when the little lines curve upward.

Smile! You'll feel great afterwards!

Tip 84

Have a Sense of Humor

People also benefit from laughter. They don't like working for people who frown and always appear too serious. Lighten up and enjoy the humor in the school setting.

Principals who can create a school culture where laughing is appreciated and accepted will realize higher performance, from adults and students both. There will also be a sense of community within the school. People will enjoy being there. But be careful how you establish your sense of humor.

Avoid sarcasm. It's destructive. Don't laugh at other people. It's okay to laugh *with* others but not *at* others. Know the fine line. Don't tease. Avoid "cute" and innocent comments that can be interpreted by people of the opposite sex to be harassment. And now you wonder, "How can a principal show a sense of humor and still avoid all these traps?" All these traps appear to be—laughable!

Ever study the masters of comedy? Those we've loved to watch over time creatively found ways to poke fun at themselves. They were the butts of their own jokes. They also mastered physical comedy, timing, and "the look." When they laughed with others, it was not at the expense of someone else. They found humor in the events around them. They turned problems into funny stories.

Simply use good judgment. Laugh, smile, and enjoy what unfolds around you.

TIP 85

Think and Behave Positively

The story goes that a retired farmer once had an older cow named Bessie that fell into an abandoned well. Despite her crying for help, the old farmer reasoned that he was too feeble, without assistance or heavy equipment, to pull her out. He had long ago sold the equipment that might have enabled him to manage such a task. Considering that the well was no longer used and the cow's advanced age, he decided to shovel it full of dirt, burying Bessie at the same time. As he tediously shoveled dirt in the well, he sadly heard old Bessie's moans. After their many good years together, he was saddened that he couldn't think of any other strategy besides doing the old cow in.

Then the moaning and crying stopped. As the dirt piled around her, Bessie had decided to stand up, shake off the dirt, and take successive steps up. After several days of shoveling, the old farmer had nearly filled the well. But Bessie, continuing to shake off her impending trouble, thinking positively, and moving up one gradual step at a time, made it to the top and walked away from what would have been her burial.

Life is all about choices. Principals can bemoan the conditions of their work or shake off their troubles and take control of their lives and careers. Look around. Complainers fall short when thinking of new strategies. When you find yourself in a "negative" situation, figure out what important information you need to glean from it, then step up on the dirt pile and walk away from it!

Bessie did it. She made a way out of no way out. So can you!

Tip 86

Show Pride and Passion for the Principalship

Pride is a motivational force. It distinguishes effective principals from others. Effective principals instill pride in their staffs. They create teams that are focused on school pride much more than their own self-interests. They have pride-building skills, tools, and techniques that help their school staff rise above the mediocre. Their core values, standards, character, courage, and commitment instill intrinsic pride in others that is much more powerful than intimidation and fear. Those with pride also have a strong work ethic, perhaps a more important characteristic for success than a superior intellect.

Everyone can develop pride in the performance of their jobs. Principals must help employees set high aspirations and see purpose in their work. They must cultivate personal relationships that develop personal trust and respect. Pride based on the relentless pursuit of a worthwhile cause helps a school improve performance. There is a fundamental correlation between pride and high-performing schools.

Pride is more than feeling good about an accomplishment. It doesn't just develop after the fact. The anticipation of feeling proud about one's (or a school's) work and performance is the more powerful motivator.

Passion should be among the many reasons one aspires to become a principal. If you can't identify it, consider another profession. If your motives are money or power, forget it. You must have the passion for learning, leading, caring, influencing the lives of others (especially students), and contributing by making a positive difference in your community.

The pressure of the job apparently sucks the passion out of some people. Perhaps they never wanted to do more than just get by. They have not found the intrinsic motivation that comes from pride and passion.

Always focus on the source of your pride and passion—student learning. Education is a noble profession. Remember what you believe in and what is worth fighting for. Let your passion and feelings show. Be a positive example for others.

People follow passionate leaders. They understand what they stand for. They are positive and exciting to be around. They focus on learning and avoid negativity. They make things happen when others cave.

8

Taking Care of Yourself

The person who does not make a choice, makes a choice.

—Jewish Proverb

Tip 87

Keep Fit

You can be the principal with the sharpest brain, keenest insights, and the highest intellect. But you won't be effective unless you also have a strong, healthy body. Effective principals are capable of many hours of productive, unrelenting work. They rarely miss school because of illness. They sleep well, eat a balanced diet, drink moderately, and engage in some form of regular exercise. There is no doubt that people who are fit move up the professional ladder faster.

Principals who are physically fit tire less easily after long days, appear happier, and suffer less from depression. They also have the energy to cook dinner for their families, coach soccer teams, attend evening activities in the school district, and become involved in their communities.

Invest in a good pair of athletic shoes. Walk or run. It's cheap. Many runners like the time of solitude for thinking. Some enjoy group runs. Enroll in yoga or kickboxing. Find your special time of day for exercise. Do what works for you.

Just do something!

Tip 88

Don't Smoke

Smokers smell! Remember the stench left in your office after a visit from a heavy, addicted smoker? That's how kids will remember the principal who smokes.

For decades, we in this country have heard antismoking messages. We know the dangers. We've seen the research. We know smoking is linked to cancer. It's dirty. It's no longer cool. Principals are well-educated people. Yet far too many continue to smoke.

If you smoke, quit. Smoking wastes time and money. Set a good example. Join a support group and work with others who are quitting. Don't offend nonsmokers by exposing your bad habit in front of them.

The principalship is demanding. It requires a strong person to persevere. Think about this. Lengthen your life. Increase the confidence and trust of the school boards and parents who place their children in your care. Do you want to be a person with good health habits or a smoker with potential medical bills and a shorter life span?

Don't smoke!

Tip 89

Develop a Winning Attitude

When people bring me the "monkeys on their backs," I can choose to display a negative and pessimistic attitude or listen, problem solve with them, delegate an action, and create a more positive and productive work climate. You can't expect teachers to do the same with students if you don't model it yourself. The principal sets the tone each day.

Leaders learn to determine if an obstacle is a roadblock or merely a bump along the way. Those who maintain positive attitudes are able to stretch themselves and model learning for others. Provide the stimulus for growth in others. Maintain a positive, winning attitude.

Tip 90

Arrive Early, Go Home Early—Even if You Take Work Home

I like to be one of the first persons to arrive at school each morning, usually between 6:30 and 7:00 a.m. Only my managing custodian and head cook typically arrive before me. The building is quiet, and I can complete many items without interruption. Usually, my custodian, cook, and I meet and talk, and we plan for the days ahead. Our special quiet time together allows for the development of a close relationship. Afterwards, I do much of my writing, planning, and e-mail communication during the thirty to forty-five minutes before other members of the staff arrive. And I can usually get to the copy machine without waiting in a line.

Once the staff begins to arrive, followed by the students at 8:35 a.m., a typical day is a whirlwind of meetings, conferences, observations, phone conversations, and interactions with people. Time flies.

I know many colleagues work late into the evening after the students and staff have gone home, but I think it is important for the principal to leave as well. I spend some solitary time, run, and lift weights. If there is still pressing work, it can be dealt with more effectively after burning off some stress (and calories).

This routine may not work for everyone. The suggestion is to recognize the value of having a life and interests away from school. Structure your day and allow time for *you*. Avoid burnout. Exercise, visit friends, volunteer at a nursing home, read, shop, do something that helps draw you away from the paperwork activities that have accumulated throughout the day. Remember to delegate.

When you retire, or worse, lie on your deathbed, it is highly unlikely that you will wish that you had spent even more hours in the office after work. Enjoy a hobby. Get another life. Take care of yourself.

9

Professional Growth

Ability is what you're capable of doing. Motivation determines what you do. Attitude determines how well you do it.

—Lou Holtz

Tip 91

Find a Mentor

Mentors love learning and growing. They also love what the protégé can become. There is passion in effective mentoring partnerships, and great mentors recognize the vitality of communicating all they know to a willing protégé.

The kind of principalship that the baby boomer generation trained for doesn't exist anymore. Societal demands and legislative expectations have added to principals' jobs and rendered them almost impossible. Change is rapid. The job is tough. The training from college and university preparatory programs is simply not enough to prepare a master teacher for the transition to the real world of the principalship. To create a successful transition, enable authentic learning and perpetual growth in a safe environment, avoid the traps, and develop a balanced plan to meet new challenges, beginning principals need mentors. Likewise, all effective principals, whatever their experience level, have trusted mentors who have guided, nurtured, supported, and listened with compassion and devotion throughout their careers.

Mentoring is a partnership. It requires a time commitment. Giving and learning is shared between mentor and protégé. An effective partnership is characterized by generosity, truth, trust, continuous communication, love of learning, acceptance, patience, devotion, passion, love, interpersonal relationship, courage, resiliency, and positive attitudes.

The success of the mentoring partnership rests with both the mentor and the protégé. It can hang on the rapport that is developed in the first encounters between them. Both need to be willing to commit to building a strong relationship, free of anxiety or fear. Principals can no longer expect to be promoted without being able to demonstrate mastery of performance standards. The protégé needs to search for a master principal, one who is receptive to learning, sharing, teaching, and reflecting. Once compatibility, rapport, and trust are established in the partnership, both mentor and protégé will work to draw the best out of each other.

Fear is a barrier to learning. Today, there is much to frighten principals. Find a mentor. Learn together. Together, all principals can lead learning communities.

Tip 92

Avoid the Status Quo Syndrome

It seems that some educators reach a plateau where they lose their passion and become fearful of change and continuous improvement. After college, they appeared to have the energy to change the profession, but what happened?

It's a matter of choice. Principals can decide to pursue new ideas, set higher goals, and value change or do the same thing year after year while waiting for retirement. When principals choose the latter, their schools become stagnant, and the learning of both students and adults levels off. Principals who want to avoid the status quo syndrome must prepare to confront their biggest leadership challenge when they find themselves with a majority of the staff resistant to change.

Most principals will say that it takes at least five or six years to accomplish major goals and effect change in a school. Once that has happened, it may be best to request a new assignment. Once you've achieved significant progress, the status quo syndrome can be hard to resist if you can't identify new challenges.

Prepare to run the race with full steam all the way to the end (retirement), or get out of the race. Children's lives are depending on you.

Tip 93

Keep Your Portfolio and Résumé Current

Take time periodically to update your résumé. It is easy to underestimate some of your most current accomplishments if you don't always update your vita as if you were applying for a new position. Over time, one can overlook many important activities and professional endeavors. And it is in the recent initiatives that a prospective employer has more interest than something that happened ten years ago.

Keep a portfolio of your work. Keep photographs, as employers love to see pictures of you in action. Show that you look like a professional in a variety of settings on typical days. Include pictures with children. They are the heart and soul of your work! Have materials that document your work and accomplishments available in hard copy formats, video, CDs, and on a Web site. Condense materials so that quality samples can inexpensively be left with a résumé.

Don't be afraid to seek a position that has more challenges and pays more money. Be up-front with your boss and make him or her aware of where and why you are seeking more challenges. You are less likely to be taken for granted in your current position if the boss thinks you have skills that someone else might want.

You might also gain a negotiation advantage to improve your current contract!

Tip 94

Develop a Professional, Collegial Network

Teaching candidates are often amazed during interviews when I mention the name of someone they know from their geographical region. I have ties to principals everywhere. Candidates also learn during the interview that I will collect opinions about their work and character using an extensive professional network. They find quickly that principals know and talk to each other.

But not all principals do. Some work in isolation. They are like teachers who prefer to shut their doors; stay to themselves; and shun the opportunities to interact, share, plan, and learn with their peers. More often than not, the performance and influence of that type of teacher is mediocre, at best. Even if they are experts in front of children, they do not contribute to their profession. Nor do like-minded principals.

Principals cannot fully develop their professional network by remaining in their schools. They must attend professional meetings, take classes, read, and visit other schools. They must know and interact with colleagues in urban, rural, suburban, and small city schools. They must broaden their horizons and awareness of issues beyond their local communities and states. They must invest in their own learning. These activities are just as important, if not more so, than being in a building managing routine events. Some of these learning opportunities will take place during school days. If principals are unwilling to leave for fear the staff cannot maintain business, instruction, and student management, they have not instilled the expectations and empowerment of others that is critical for daily operation.

My observations of principals attending professional meetings or conferences remind me of my experiences at junior high school dances. There were those who were always first on the dance floor, knew all the latest moves, and seemed to have the most fun. And there were others who sat watching in chairs along the wall. They never seemed to enjoy themselves or learn to dance. They waited all night for invitations that never developed. Those who were aggressive and developed their own dance groups learned skills that enabled them to be successful in later social settings. They knew that to enjoy the dance, they had to dance. They took action and got involved. They didn't sit by themselves.

The principal who fails to develop a network becomes the proverbial lone wolf—the runt, outcast, or rebel of the pack among colleagues. Lone wolves travel across thousands of miles of dangerous terrain suffering painful rejections from numerous packs. They are fortunate when they find a pack that will accept them. Life becomes easier. Survival becomes a shared activity.

There are forces at work that encourage principals to become lone wolves. They know they can further destroy what they don't like about public education by dispersing the pack. To persevere and to survive, principals must stay together.

There is no "I" in *teamwork*. The greatest teams in sports history have been those where players and coaches committed to common goals, recognized the value of each other's contributions, and achieved together. Principals can learn by observing wolf packs, middle school dances, and athletic teams at work.

Networking for professional growth, and our survival, must become one of your most important activities. The excuse of being too busy is folly. Never fail to invest in your professional development. Communicate with those who do what you do, and become a member of the team.

Tip 95

Read

Reading is fundamental. Principals want every child to learn to read and to enjoy a lifetime of reading. It is highly improbable that nonreaders can enjoy an easy life in a world where knowledge is expanding at record speed.

Principals must read. To remain current, they must read the professional journals of the leading professional associations. They must understand laws. Read magazines about current events. Read the newspapers. Reading books expands the mind and enables the learner to gain new insights. Read for enjoyment and relaxation.

Just like making time for fitness, principals must find time to read. Even though most activities of a principal's day involve reading, quiet, reflective time away from the interruptions of the office is best for developing the special time for reading. Share good titles and articles with colleagues, and encourage others to share their insights from books with you.

Reading principals are more inquisitive, knowledgeable, and well rounded than their colleagues who are "too busy" to read. Readers have thoughts to share in conversations. They think more critically. Reading principals practice what they preach. They model adult learning. They set the tone for their school.

TIP 96

Write

Just as they must model the importance of reading for all learners, principals must also write. But for many, this is more difficult. Enrolling in an advanced degree program is a proven way to improve one's writing skills. If not that, there are many seminars and workshops that focus on writing. Just like learning to read, one becomes a better writer by practicing.

Principals engage in many writing activities in their jobs: writing newsletters, grants, proposals, letters, memos, staff bulletins, and so on. But these activities become routine. I am suggesting that principals extend themselves beyond their job requirements and write reflectively about their work, how they feel, what they think, what they need, and document their thinking about the principalship so that they can share it with colleagues. By writing, people really learn to reflect. They become more advanced critical readers and thinkers. They expand themselves. Others can learn from your insights.

Some think they have nothing valuable to share. They can't think of anything to write about. Sound familiar? Would we accept that excuse from students?

I won't either. Principals, grab your pens and start writing!

Tip 97

Improve Your Speaking Skills

The most effective principals are successful talkers. Sounds simple, but it's true. Throughout time, most successful people have been successful talkers: for instance, Oprah Winfrey, Walter Cronkite, Martin Luther King, and Nelson Mandela. Consider our most successful presidents, politicians, media figures, entertainers, and leaders from various walks of life: The most memorable and influential learned to speak well in different settings to achieve success and even greatness. The same is true for principals.

Those principals who fear public speaking, develop sweaty palms when answering questions in the spotlight, or can't convey their thoughts to others can develop skills that will make them better talkers. Not everyone has to be a spellbinder, but principals must be effective talkers in everyday conversations in the school setting, social gatherings, and their communities.

Talk show host Larry King suggests the best talkers have things in common. Principals who are great talkers share the following communication characteristics:

- They talk about issues with people who hold different points of view.
- They persuasively convey knowledge and opinions about a wide variety of issues using language levels understood by the listener.

- They are passionate and enthusiastic.
- They don't talk about themselves all the time. They listen.
- They are curious.
- They empathize.
- They have a sense of humor.
- They have their own styles of talking.

Some principals speak softly while others are dramatic. Some are compelling when they speak, others bombastic, while many know how to tug on the heart. Styles can be further described as aggressive, laid back, curious, intense, passive, or aloof. There are diverse, rich regional dialects. There are numerous examples of different talking styles, and effective principals perfect the style that works best for them. And the most brilliant talkers know when it is best to remain silent.

Principals who are the best talkers model appropriate speech standards. They pronounce words correctly, use correct verb tenses, avoid ending sentences with prepositions, employ contrast in their lines of speech, and choose to simplify rather than inflate the complexity of the words they use. They avoid trendy talk, jargon, and buzzwords. They also know that certain sounds, words, and oral crutches add nothing to a conversation. The best example of an oral crutch is "you know;" used in excess, it can cause listeners to miss the message of the speaker. Good talkers also avoid "uh" "um," and "OK." In addition, "basically," "hopefully" or "whatever" are filler words that add nothing to a conversation. Today's younger generation uses the word "like" a lot, another filler word that dates them and leaves some conversations unintelligible.

Some people dismiss these habits as harmless. Principals who are the best talkers know better. They listen to themselves, sometimes even recording or videotaping for later reflection. Effective principals self-analyze. They seek feedback. Some practice in front of mirrors. They know their effectiveness rests on how others perceive their style on the public address system, in meetings, in front of large groups, and in intimate one-on-one conversations. They seek a critical friend who listens and helps with continuous improvement and reflection.

College courses do little to prepare an aspiring principal for the conversational necessities of the real world. Talking is the activity that absorbs the most time of a principal's day. Despite experience, it can be challenging. Principals who are the best communicators continuously work to be confident and effective in any situation. They know they must be able to get listeners on their side and get their messages across.

Tip 98

Give Professional Presentations

In the very last tip, it is suggested that you join state and national professional associations. Once your registration is completed, start becoming active in those associations by sharing an idea or best practice with others at a professional workshop or conference. Be alive, active, and know your audience. Tell them things they need to learn. Be authentic. Entertain.

My trombone teacher always said that I would learn more about playing the instrument when I taught it to someone else rather than just playing by myself. He was right! Preparing to teach, writing lesson plans, writing a speech, and preparing a concurrent session for a professional conference are all valuable learning experiences. You really master the material when you teach it to another. Learn to do it well. Share authentic experiences and stories. Help people learn from your experience and implement your ideas in their work.

It is flattering to be asked to present, and it is a professional compliment when someone else "borrows" your ideas for their school. Many of the best ideas and practices in schools are those that have been shared and passed around through numerous professional conferences.

Do it! Submit a proposal today. Everyone has something to share. Most professional associations have their requests for proposals online. I hope to see you there!

Tip 99

Collaborate With Colleagues

It won't serve you well to be the Lone Ranger with your colleagues. Unless you are the only elementary or middle level principal in your school district, you will find other colleagues you will need to work with. Working against them will make your professional life very lonely, as they will eventually cast you aside. You will also get left behind with a reputation of being difficult!

Does collaboration mean you can't compete? No. It means you talk, plan, and share ideas. You support each other and commiserate. You share best practices. You shoulder the responsibility for projects together. It is always a compliment to see an idea you've had in place at your school being replicated in another. A professional level of competition and teamwork makes for a healthy, progressive atmosphere.

Organize regular meetings of your colleagues. Have the business meetings on school time. Focus on issues. Take the initiative as leaders. Great things happen when people work together. Two or more heads are better than one.

Tip 100

Invest in Professional Attire

If the future of my career were being held in the balance in a courtroom, I would want to be represented by the best available lawyer. In my mind, that man or woman would be impeccably groomed and dressed in a professional, well-tailored suit while pleading my case. If I were lying on a hospital gurney heading toward surgery, I would want to see my doctor properly outfitted and sanitized for the task at hand. I expect to find food service personnel with clean hands and hair collected so that it stays out of my food.

I also expect principals to be dressed as professionals. So does the public.

We dress particular ways to play football, dance, or play in an orchestra. Yet some principals fail to dress for school. In most areas, dress codes for teachers are lenient and difficult to enforce. If teachers choose not to look like professionals, should principals do the same?

One morning several years ago, an angry parent told me how upset she was, having just witnessed the custodian walk past a child who had just vomited in the hallway. When she described the custodian as being male, I told her my managing custodian was female. It didn't take me long to realize that she had mistakenly identified an unkempt teacher in jeans and T-shirt as the custodian.

I've visited schools where it was difficult to pick out the principal. Others have shared with me that they don't wear ties, jackets, dresses, or suits because they don't want to intimidate their parents who live in poverty. Contrary to that thinking, I suggest that people of all socioeconomic groups will give their respect to the person who is appropriately dressed as a principal.

Schools exist to perpetuate the middle class. Their mission is to acclimate *all* students to achieve success in the middle-class world. Principals set the tone for their schools. Dress first class.

Know the norms of your community. People dress differently for professional work in Hawaii than in Minnesota. But they still have professional standards. Don't flaunt but raise that standard. People will remember the way you look, the perfume or cologne you wear, and the image you create.

Unless there is a special event or activity that implies different attire, dress like a professional. The principal's job is the most important work in your community.

Tip 101

Join Your State and National Professional Associations

One of the first things beginning principals should know and do after signing a contract is to join both the state and national professional associations for principals. Yearly membership is open anytime. Membership information for the National Association of Elementary School Principals can be found by visiting www.naesp.org, where one can also find links to most state associations. Those who ignore this tip often find themselves alienated from their colleagues, unaware of best practice, and isolated in the profession.

The professional materials in the form of magazines, monthly mailings, Web resources, legal updates, and liability insurance benefits make membership a bargain. Many school districts assume the costs incurred for principals' professional memberships and professional development. Where that is not the case, colleagues should negotiate for that benefit.

Both the state and national associations annually provide professional development conferences tailored specifically to meet the needs of elementary and middle level principals. All attendees benefit from opportunities to discuss their craft, learn from experts, network, and share best practices. In addition, state and national principal associations provide ongoing, regional workshops and conferences developed by practicing principals for practicing principals.

The principalship is ever changing, with increasing demands. The principal's day is never the same. Learning never stops. It makes sense to develop connections, share, and learn from others in the field.

The Principals' Creed

We are dedicated to ensuring that every child in America receives a quality education.

We care about our country by caring deeply about its children.

We believe that no barrier should separate a child from the best education a school can offer . . . that neither race nor sex nor ethnic heritage nor geography nor social or economic status may be used to deny a child the opportunity to acquire a solid foundation in reading, writing, and mathematics . . . in critical thinking . . . and in values of friendship, compassion, honesty, and self-esteem.

We are committed to instructional excellence and we support the aspirations of teachers everywhere to give each boy and girl a quality school experience during the crucial years of childhood.

We accept the challenge of the research showing that quality education in every school depends on the expertise, dedication, and leadership of the principal of that school.

Affirmed by the National Association of Elementary School Principals. Reprinted with permission.

Suggested Readings

Bell, C. R. (2002). *Managers as mentors: Building partnerships for learning.* San Francisco: Berrett-Koehler.

Bennis, W., & Thomas, R. (2002). *Geeks and geezers.* Boston: Harvard Business School Press.

BenShea, N. (2000). *What every principal would like to say . . . and what to say next time.* Thousand Oaks, CA: Corwin.

Blanchard, K. (2002). *Whale done! The power of positive relationships.* New York: Free Press.

Blanchard, K., & Bowles, S. (1993). *Raving fans.* New York: William Morrow.

Blanchard, K., Oncken, W., & Burrows, H. (1989). *The one-minute manager meets the monkey.* New York: Quill William Morrow.

Blaydes, J. (2003). *The educator's book of quotes.* Thousand Oaks, CA: Corwin.

Daresh, J. C. (2002). *What it means to be a principal.* Thousand Oaks, CA: Corwin.

Fowler, C. (1996). *Strong arts, strong schools.* New York: Oxford University Press.

Fox, J. (1998). *How to become CEO.* New York: Hyperion.

Frase, L., & Streshly, W. (2000). *Top ten myths in education.* Lanham, MD: Scarecrow.

Fullan, M. (1997). *What's worth fighting for in the principalship.* New York: Teachers College Press.

Gladwell, M. (2000). *The tipping point: How little things can make a big difference.* Boston: Little, Brown.

Grant, J., & Forsten, C. (1999). *If you're riding a horse and it dies, get off.* Peterborough, NH: Crystal Springs.

Guiliani, R. (2002). *Leadership.* New York: Hyperion.

Johnson, S. (1998). *Who moved my cheese?* New York: Putnam.

Katzenbach, J. R. (2003). *Why pride matters more than money.* New York: Crown.

King, L. (1994). *How to talk to anyone, anytime, anywhere: The secrets of good communication.* New York: Three Rivers.

Kosmoski, G., & Pollack, D. (2000). *Managing difficult, frustrating, and hostile conversations.* Thousand Oaks, CA: Corwin.

Littauer, F. (1999). *How to get along with difficult people.* Eugene, OR: Harvest House.

Marx, G. (2000). *Ten trends: Educating children for a profoundly different future.* Arlington, VA: Educational Research Service.

Maxwell, J. (1995). *Developing the leaders around you.* Nashville, TN: Injoy.

Maxwell, J. (1995). *Leadership 101.* Nashville, TN: Thomas Nelson.

McEwan, E. (1998). *How to deal with parents who are angry, troubled, afraid, or just plain crazy.* Thousand Oaks, CA: Corwin.

McKain, S. (2002). *All business is show business.* Nashville, TN: Rutledge Hill.

National Association of Elementary School Principals. (2001). *Leading learning communities: Standards for what principals should know and be able to do.* Alexandria, VA: Author.

Parker, D. (2003). *Confident communication.* Thousand Oaks, CA: Corwin.

Payne, R. (2001). *A framework for understanding poverty.* Highlands, TX: aha! Process.

Quaglia, R., & Quay, S. (2003). *Changing lives through the principalship.* Alexandria VA: National Association of Elementary School Principals.

Schumaker, D., & Sommers, W. (2001). *Being a successful principal.* Thousand Oaks, CA: Corwin.

Towery, T. (1995). *The wisdom of the wolves.* Naperville, IL: Sourcebooks.

Whitaker, T. (1999). *Dealing with difficult teachers.* Larchmont, NY: Eye on Education.

Young, P. (2002, November/December). Can you hear that sound? *Principal 82(2),* 68.

Young, P. (2002, September/October). Monkeys in our schools. *Today's School 3(2),* 34–36.

Young, P., & Sheets, J. (2003). *Mastering the art of mentoring principals.* Arlington, VA: KGE.

Young, P., Sheets, J., & Kesner, R. (2003, May/June). Mentoring new principals: Two perspectives. *Principal 82(5),* 48–51.

Young, P., Sheets, J., & Knight, D. (2004). *Mentoring principals.* Thousand Oaks, CA: Corwin.

CORWIN PRESS

The Corwin Press logo—a raven striding across an open book—represents the union of courage and learning. Corwin Press is committed to improving education for all learners by publishing books and other professional development resources for those serving the field of K–12 education. By providing practical, hands-on materials, Corwin Press continues to carry out the promise of its motto: **"Helping Educators Do Their Work Better."**

NAESP

NATIONAL ASSOCIATION OF ELEMENTARY SCHOOL PRINCIPALS
Serving All Elementary and Middle Level Principals

National Association of Elementary School Principals
1615 Duke Street, Alexandria, VA 22314-3483
E-mail: naesp@naesp.org. Web site: www.naesp.org

The 29,500 members of the National Association of Elementary School Principals provide administrative and instructional leadership for public and private elementary and middle schools throughout the United States, Canada, and overseas. Founded in 1921, NAESP is today a vigorously independent professional association with its own headquarters building in Alexandria, Virginia, just across the Potomac River from the nation's capital. From this special vantage point, NAESP conveys the unique perspective of the elementary and middle school principal to the highest policy councils of our national government. Through national and regional meetings, award-winning publications, and joint efforts with its 50 state affiliates, NAESP is a strong advocate both for its members and for the 33 million American children enrolled in preschool, kindergarten, and grades 1 through 8.